# 101 WAYS TO PAY LESS TAX

2015 - 2016 £ TAX YEAR

**Ashley Smith** FCCA CTA ATT
**Iain Watson**
**Hugh Williams**

101 Ways to Pay Less Tax
by Ashley Smith, Iain Watson and Hugh Williams

1st edition 2005
2nd edition 2006
3rd edition 2007
4th edition 2008
5th edition 2009
6th edition 2010
7th edition 2011
8th edition 2012
9th edition 2013
10th edition 2014
11th edition 2015

Lawpack Publishing Limited
76–89 Alscot Road,
London SE1 3AW

www.lawpack.co.uk

ISBN: 9781910143193
Ebook ISBN: 9781910143209

MIX
Paper from
responsible sources
FSC® C011748

**Exclusion of Liability and Disclaimer**

While every effort has been made to ensure that this Lawpack publication provides accurate and expert guidance, it is impossible to predict all the circumstances in which it may be used. Accordingly, neither the publisher, authors, retailer, nor any other suppliers shall be liable to any person or entity with respect to any loss or damage caused or alleged to be caused by the information contained in or omitted from this Lawpack publication.

# Contents

# About the authors

**Ashley Smith** FCCA CTA ATT is the proprietor of H M Williams Chartered Certified Accountants.

**Iain Watson** is Tax Manager at H M Williams; formerly with H M Revenue & Customs, he offers an invaluable insider's view of tax legislation.

**Hugh Williams** was Senior Partner at H M Williams until his retirement in December 2014. He founded the practice in 1973 and has written a number of professional and consumer books on tax and law. His retirement allows him more time with his family, but he still retains a keen interest in financial and political matters.

Representing H M Williams, the authors have been awarded the 2020 trophy for the most innovative medium-sized UK firm of accountants. They have also been winners of the prestigious Butterworth Tolley Best Small to Medium-Sized UK Tax Team Award. And in addition, the firm was also awarded the coveted *Daily Telegraph*/Energis Customer Service Award in the Professional and Business Services, Small Organisation category.

'The hardest thing in the world to understand is Income Tax.'
Albert Einstein

# Important facts

Welcome to *101 Ways to Pay Less Tax*. It's packed with information and advice on your obligations and rights as a taxpayer.

The information this book contains has been carefully compiled from professional sources, but its accuracy is not guaranteed, as laws and regulations may change in the Budget and be subject to changing interpretations. Please be aware that the tax rates and allowances included in this book are those that were announced by the Chancellor of the Exchequer in his Budget of 18 March 2015 and the Summer Budget of 8 July 2015.

Tax regulations are stated as at 6 April 2015.

Neither this nor any other publication can take the place of an accountant on important tax matters. Common sense should determine whether you need the assistance of an accountant rather than relying solely on the information in *101 Ways to Pay Less Tax*.

# CHAPTER 1
# General principles

1. Working Tax Credits
2. Child Tax Credits
3. Universal Credit
4. Use an accountant
5. Pay tax on time
6. The fundamentals of tax planning

Although this may appear to be the wrong foot on which to start a book about saving tax, you should never put sound commercial judgement after saving tax. In other words, it's nearly always the case that it's better to make money and pay tax than to pay no tax but make no money.

Never let the tax tail wag the common sense dog.

## 1 Working Tax Credits

Working Tax Credits are payable whether or not you have children. So if you have no children or only adult children, don't assume that tax credits are not for you; they could be if your income is low enough. You will receive payments directly from HM Revenue & Customs (HMRC).

There are several different parts of the credit, which are paid depending on marital status, the hours worked, your age and whether or not you are disabled. Because of this, there is no 'one size fits all' illustration. If you are in doubt, it's always best to submit a protective claim (i.e. you can withdraw it later if you subsequently want to) as tax credits are only backdated for three months. This can be done online at gov.uk/browse/benefits/tax-credits or you can contact HMRC's Tax Credits Helpline on 0345 300 3900 and ask for a claim form. Tax Credit calculators are also available on the website (and others) and by working through them you will have a guide to how much you may be able to claim.

## 2 Child Tax Credits

As with Working Tax Credits, there are various elements to be taken into account. Given the range of variables affecting eligibility, we recommend visiting the HMRC website (www.gov.uk/browse/benefits/tax-credits-calculator) and completing their Tax Credits Calculator. It's worth making a protective claim even if your income slightly exceeds the limit, as circumstances can change

##  3 Universal Credit

Universal Credit a new benefit that has started to replace six existing benefits with a single monthly payment. It will eventually replace:

- Income-based Jobseeker's Allowance

- Income-related Employment and Support Allowance

- Income Support

- Working Tax Credit

- Child Tax Credit

- Housing Benefit

Your eligibility to claim Universal Credit depends on where you live and your personal circumstances.

Universal Credit started to be introduced in stages, from April 2013. It will become increasingly available across Great Britain over the coming 12 to 24 months. New claims to existing benefits, which Universal Credit is replacing, will continue to close down, with the vast majority of claimants moving onto Universal Credit during 2016 and 2017.

The purpose is to simplify the benefit system and make it easier for people to take jobs, even for brief periods, without running the risk of losing out financially.

Universal Credit will not replace: Attendance Allowance, Bereavement benefits, Child Benefit, Carer's Allowance, Council Tax Benefit, Maternity Allowance, Statutory Maternity Pay, Statutory Sick Pay, Disability Living Allowance, Contributory Employment Support Allowance, Contributory Jobseekers Allowance, Pension Credit, Industrial Injuries Disablement benefit, Personal Independence Payment and War Pensions.

Universal Credit will be paid on a monthly basis to a household, regardless of whether the household comprises one individual, a couple or a family. There is a main element plus additional elements which have to be applied for if a household qualifies. These elements are: Child and Disabled Child Element, Childcare Element, Carer Element, Limited Capability for Work Element and Housing Element.

Universal Credit will have a cap applied to make it impossible for people to get more by claiming benefits than the average net weekly wage. For a household this figure is £500 per week and for single adults the cap is £350 per week. The childcare element of the Universal Credit will be excluded from the benefit cap.

Some households will be exempt from the benefit cap i.e. those households where Disability Living Allowance or Attendance Allowance are claimed.

One of the major changes being introduced is that, with a few exceptions, all claimants will have to enter into a binding commitment that in exchange for receiving Universal Credit they undertake to look for and take on any work that is available.

There is a lot of 'small print' related to what jobs have to be accepted and there are also going to be sanctions for those who do not comply with their commitment in this regard.

Concerns have been expressed by certain groups about this new legislation, but equally, the huge cost of paying benefits has to be reined in; so that only the most needy and deserving are protected, and those who can work should be encouraged and supported to do so

##  4 Use an accountant

A qualified accountant will know a lot about what your legal obligations are in terms of taxation and will also know lots of ways to legitimately keep your liabilities to a minimum. Generally speaking, your accountant will save you tax better than if you were dealing with matters yourself, and your accountant's fees may be less than the savings you are making. Provided you do as your accountant asks, you also have the peace of mind of knowing that you have complied with your legal obligations.

##  5 Pay tax on time

Always pay any tax you owe on time. Interest is charged on late payment at an annualised rate of three per cent. At current rates, even if you have your money in a high-interest account, it's probably better to pay HMRC on time. However, if you are going to go overdrawn by paying HMRC, particularly if you don't have an authorised facility, then it may be cheaper to pay interest to HMRC than it is to pay interest to your bank.

If your balancing payment (not your payment on account) for any given year is paid more than 30 days late, there will be a surcharge of five per cent of the tax still owed; a further five per cent will be charged on any sums still not paid five months later, and another five per cent on anything still owing eleven months after that.

Therefore, if you have to make a balancing payment and a payment on account on 31 January, and you don't have sufficient funds to pay in full, endeavour to settle the balancing payment element by the end of February.

As a general rule, if you owe HMRC money and are unable to pay, you will generally get more favourable treatment by discussing the matter with HMRC's staff rather than burying your head in the sand and avoiding the issue. It has a dedicated telephone number (the Business Payments Support Service) for businesses that are struggling to pay their tax on time: 0300 200 3835.

In recent years, much emphasis has been placed on 'fairness' and 'paying the right amount of tax'. HMRC has significantly strengthened the tax collection side of its operations, based on perceived public support for this and also the need to collect as much of what is due as possible due to the current financial state of the country.

From the date of Royal Assent for the 2015 Summer Budget, HMRC will have the power to raid the bank accounts of people and businesses who have persistently refused to pay the tax they owe, even though they can afford to do so. This is a controversial development and HMRC has advised that safeguards will be put in place. We remain very concerned about this, as HMRC has demonstrated on many occasions that it doesn't always get things right. This process will only be used for debts in excess of £1,000, where the individual has an aggregate credit of at least £5,000.

 ## 6 The fundamentals of tax planning

All taxpayers have the right to arrange their affairs under the law to minimise their liability to tax. This can be done either by choosing a commercial option which generates a lower tax bill than another, or by organising your financial affairs in such a way so as to minimise the tax bill. While there is nothing wrong with using arrangements set up for no other purpose than to avoid tax, it should be borne in mind that such arrangements may not necessarily be in your wider interest, as we have already said. If you participate in any specialised tax avoidance schemes, a declaration to this effect must be made on your Tax Return.

The terms 'avoidance' and 'evasion' are very different in meaning, but the media and certain politicians seem to view them as much the same. Legislation continues to be introduced to make it more difficult to participate and gain a tax advantage from these specialised schemes.

# CHAPTER 2
# For those with low incomes

**7.** Become a foster carer

**8.** Claim tax back on any interest you receive

## 7 Become a foster carer

There is an exemption from tax if you provide foster care to children and young people who are placed with you by local authorities (Health and Social Care Trusts in Northern Ireland) or independent fostering providers. The first £10,000 plus £200 per week for each child aged under 11 (£250 for over 11s) is tax free. If the amounts you receive exceed these limits, you can choose between paying tax on the excess or on the gross receipts less expenses. This exemption doesn't apply to private fostering arrangements.

If you are an adult placement carer in a scheme recognised by the National Association of Adult Placement Services (NAAPS), there are simplified arrangements for calculating your taxable profit. To qualify, you have to provide accommodation and full-time care for between one and three adults, or respite care. The first option is to claim 'rent a room' relief (see number 84). The second option is the fixed-expenses method, whereby you deduct fixed expenses for the adults in your care. These amount to £400 per week for the first adult and £250 for the second and third adults. Any amount you receive over and above this is taxable. However, if the fixed expenses exceed your income, you can't claim loss relief.

Remember, whether you foster an adult or child, you are self-employed and may have to pay National Insurance Contributions. However, as explained in number 45, it may be worthwhile paying them even if you do not have to do so, to protect your National Insurance contribution record.

## 8 Claim tax back on any interest you receive

Don't pay tax if you don't have to. If your bank or building society is deducting tax from interest and your income is less than:

* £10,600 if you were born on or after 6 April 1948;
* £10,660 if you were born before 6 April 1938;

you should register to receive gross interest. This is quite straightforward. All you have to do is ask your bank or building society for Form R85 ('Getting your interest without tax taken off') or download one from

HMRC's website, fill it in and sign it. If the account is in joint names of husband and wife and only one spouse pays tax, the non-taxpaying spouse can receive gross interest on 50 per cent of the interest.

If your income exceeds the above limits by no more than £5,000 and includes interest, you are not liable to pay tax on the interest, but the bank or building society has to deduct tax at 20 per cent. You can then reclaim the excess by filling in Form R40 (available from your local tax office or on the HMRC website at www.hmrc.gov.uk).

From 6 April 2015, the starting rate for savings income will be 0 per cent and the maximum amount of taxable savings income that can be eligible for this starting rate is £5,000.

See also tip number 84 about renting out a room in your main residence. This can be a useful way of supplementing your income without any tax implications.

# CHAPTER 3
# For those with high incomes

## 9 Enterprise Investment Scheme (EIS)

Relief from Income Tax is available when a *qualifying individual* subscribes for *eligible shares* in a *qualifying company* carrying on (or intending to carry on) a *qualifying trade*.

Now, let's look at what this actually means ...

A *qualifying individual* is someone who is not connected with the company, which excludes past or present employees and certain directors, and anyone who controls more than 30 per cent of the capital.

*Eligible shares* are new ordinary shares issued for cash.

A *qualifying company* is an unquoted trading company, which can include companies quoted on the Alternative Investment Market (AIM) and which carries on its business activity wholly or mainly within the UK. The company must not have plans to become quoted; in addition, the assets of the company must not exceed £15 million immediately before the issue of shares or £16 million immediately after the issue of shares.

A *qualifying trade* is broadly anything that doesn't include, to any substantial extent, the following: accountancy services, legal services, finance, banking, insurance, farming, market gardening, property development, forestry and timber production, leasing, letting, or operating or managing hotels, guest houses, nursing and residential care homes, and businesses entitled to receive renewable energy feed in tariffs.

HM Revenue & Customs (HMRC) will give advance (provisional) approval that the shares will qualify for relief, but that relief will only be due when an EIS3 Certificate has been received from the company.

Investments can be made of any amount up to a maximum of £1 million in any tax year. Both husbands and wives have their own limit. The whole amount subscribed for can be carried back to the previous year and claimed as if the investment had been made in that year.

Income Tax relief is given at 30 per cent when calculating the investor's tax liability for the year.

If the shares are sold less than three years after they were acquired, then the Income Tax relief is lost. Furthermore, if the investor 'receives value' during the three years, then relief is also lost. There are a number of ways in which an individual can 'receive value' (e.g. by repaying or writing off a debt, making loans or providing other benefits), but this doesn't include the payment of dividends that don't exceed a normal return on investment.

##  10 Seed Enterprise Investment Scheme

This scheme, launched on 6 April 2012, is similar to the existing Enterprise Investment Scheme, but is aimed specifically at small, start-up businesses. The underlying purpose of this is to help stimulate entrepreneurship and kick-start the economy.

The company receiving the investment must be carrying on, or preparing to carry on, a new business in a 'qualifying trade' (the definition of this is the same as for the EIS – see above). The company must have fewer than 25 employees and have assets of less than £200,000. The subscriber can invest up to £100,000 in a single tax year with unused amounts being available to be carried back to a previous year, as under the existing EIS rules. The overall maximum investment in each company is £150,000.

The investor must own less than 30 per cent of the business and the business must be a UK company. The best bit is that 50 per cent tax relief is given on the investment, regardless of the investor's marginal rate of tax.

##  11 Venture Capital Trusts (VCTs)

These are, in simple terms, quoted companies that hold EIS-style investments. The investor is still investing in new and expanding companies but not directly, and therefore has less risk.

Tax relief is due when the shares are subscribed for. The maximum investment in any tax year is £200,000. The rate of relief is 30 per cent for 2015/16.

Dividends from ordinary shares in VCTs are exempt from Income Tax provided that shares equal in total to not more than the annual investment limit are acquired in each tax year. The ten per cent tax credit attached to share dividends is not repayable, but any higher-rate tax liability on the dividends is avoided.

Provided that the shares have been held for at least five years, when the shares are sold at a profit there is no liability to Capital Gains Tax.

## 12 Community Investment Tax Relief

The scheme encourages investment in disadvantaged communities by allowing tax relief to individuals and companies which invest through Community Development Finance Institutions (CDFIs). The CDFIs will then invest in businesses and social and community enterprises in under-invested areas. The relief available is 25 per cent of the investment spread over five years (five per cent per year). The investment must be held for a minimum of five years, otherwise the relief may be reduced or withdrawn. There is no upper limit on the amount that can be invested, but there are limits on the amount that can be raised by the CDFIs and that maximum cannot be exceeded.

## 13 Maximise pension contributions

You get relief at your highest rate of tax for pension contributions. Therefore, if you are a higher-rate or additional-rate taxpayer, it's even more important that you maximise your contributions. You can get tax relief on contributions up to 100 per cent of your annual earnings (up to an annual allowance set at £40,000 from 6 April 2014). So, if you put £100 into your pension scheme, the tax relief the government gives you on that is worth at least £25. Even if you are not a taxpayer, you can still get tax relief on pension contributions. You can put in up to £2,880 in any one tax year and the government will top this up with another £720 – giving you total pension savings with tax relief of £3,600 per year.

If your pension pot is more than the 'lifetime allowance' when you come to take your pension, you may be subject to a tax charge at that time. But this will only apply if your total pension savings are in excess of £1.25 million (reducing to £1 million from 6 April 2016).

You cannot take a pension before you are 55. There are a couple of exceptions: you will still be able to retire early due to poor health, and if you have the right to retire before 50 at 6 April 2006, that right may be protected.

Pension contributions can also be useful for those with incomes between £100,000 and £121,200. People with incomes in this bracket will find that because of the vagaries of the tax system, the band above £100,000 will be taxed at the staggering rate of 62 per cent. Possibly the easiest way to avoid this trap is to make additional contributions into a pension scheme.

Similarly, pension contributions can be used to reduce income to below the critical £50,000 to £60,000 band where Child Benefit is lost. When contemplating making pension contributions, as with any other investment, it's always important to take good professional advice.

The 2014 Budget proposed radical changes to pensions from April 2015, primarily with regard to abolishing the need to purchase an annuity with your pension funds. A pledge was also made to give everyone free financial advice on the options available to them when they come to draw on their pension funds. Some commentators questioned whether people could be trusted to spend their pension funds wisely. It is the authors' view that professional independent financial advice should be taken when considering how to finance retirement.

- The commutation limit is being increased from £18,000 to £30,000. The legislation provides for trivial benefits to be commuted and paid as a one-off lump sum payment once you have reached the age of 60, but have not reached age 75. This can be done only if the value of your benefit entitlement under all registered pension schemes, along with all rights that have previously crystallised for lifetime allowance purposes (including any pensions in payment on 5 April 2006), do not exceed a maximum value (the commutation limit) as valued on a specific date (the nominated date).

- The capped drawdown limit is being increased from 120 per cent to 150 per cent of an equivalent annuity. Capped drawdown is a form of 'income withdrawal' where your pension is paid direct from the funds in your pension scheme. Within certain limits you can choose how much pension you can get each year. You can change the amount you receive each year.

- The £20,000 flexible drawdown threshold is being reduced to £12,000. Flexible drawdown is a form of income withdrawal', where your pension is paid direct from your pension scheme. There is no limit on the amount that your pension scheme can pay you in any year. You can take as much or as little as you like. If you want to, you can take out all the funds in your arrangement as one payment. All payments of flexible drawdown are taxed under PAYE. Not everyone can take flexible drawdown. In particular you must be getting a minimum amount of secure pension income (£12,000) every year to qualify for flexible drawdown.

- The small pots limit is being increased from £2,000 to £10,000. You must be at least 60 years of age to take your pension pot as a lump sum. The number of small pots which can be taken as a lump sum is increased from two to three.

## 14 Use all of your pension allowance

As mentioned in the previous point, there is now a cap on the total amount you can put into a pension in any given tax year (£40,000 for 2015/16). However, you can increase this if you have not used up all of your allowance, by carrying forward any unused allowance from the previous three years into the current tax year. You only get penalised on any amount of pension savings in excess of the total of:

- the annual allowance for the tax year;
- any unused annual allowance you carry forward from the previous three years;

However, you can only carry forward unused annual allowance if, during that tax year, you were in either:

- a registered UK pension scheme; or
- an overseas pension scheme and either you or your employer qualified for UK tax relief on pension savings in that scheme.

There is also a strict order in which you can use up your annual allowance. First, you use the annual allowance from the current tax year, followed by any unused annual allowance from the previous three tax years, using the earliest tax year first.

## 15 What income is free from tax?

- Adoption Allowances
- Adult Placement Carers' Income
- Annuities from gallantry awards
- Attendance Allowance
- Bereavement Payments

- Betting, lottery and pools winnings, and raffle prizes
- Car parking benefits
- Child Benefit
- Child dependency additions
- Child Tax Credit
- Child Trust Funds
- Children's Savings Accounts (Junior ISAs)
- Christmas bonuses paid by the state to pensioners
- Compensation for loss of employment of up to £30,000 (professional advice must be sought)
- Compensation for mis-sold personal pensions
- Compensation paid to Equitable Life Policyholders
- Council Tax Benefit
- Damages and compensation for personal injury, including interest
- Disability Living Allowance
- Educational Maintenance Allowance
- Electricity microgeneration for home use
- Foster Care Income
- Gifts for employees from third parties if they are under £250 a year
- Gratuities and bounties from the armed forces
- Guardian's Allowance
- Home improvement, repair and insulation grants
- Housing Benefit
- Incapacity Benefit (short term – lower rate)
- Income Support
- Individual Savings Accounts (ISAs)
- Industrial injury benefits
- Insurance bond withdrawals of up to five per cent per year (this can be complicated and professional advice should be sought)
- Insurance policy payments (e.g. mortgage payment protection, permanent health)
- Interest from National Savings Certificates
- Interest on late paid pension contributions
- Interest on overpaid tax
- Interest on over-repayment of student loans
- Invalidity pensions
- Jobfinder's Grant
- Life assurance policy bonuses and profits
- Long-service awards of up to £50 for each year of service (for employees)
- Lump sums from an approved pension scheme
- Maintenance or alimony payments
- Maternity Allowance
- Miners' Coal Allowance

- National Savings Certificates' increase in value
- Pension Credit
- Pensions from Austria or Germany to victims of Nazi persecution
- Premium bond prizes
- Provident benefits paid by a trade union of up to £4,000 for lump-sum payments
- Purchased life annuities – capital element only
- Rent-a-room income up to £4,250 a year
- Save As You Earn (SAYE) schemes bonuses and interest
- Scholarship income and bursaries
- Severe Disablement Allowances
- Share option profits made under an SAYE option scheme – Capital Gains Tax may be payable
- Shares awarded under an approved Share Incentive Plan (professional advice must be sought)
- Social fund payments
- Statutory Redundancy Pay
- Strike and unemployment pay from a trade union
- Student Grants
- Suggestion scheme awards
- Training allowances for reserve forces
- Travel to work on a works bus
- TV licence payment
- Vaccine damage payment
- Venture Capital Trust dividends
- War Disablement Benefits
- War Widows' Pension
- Winter fuel payments
- Woodlands
- Working Tax Credit

##  16  Pension contributions and the over 55s

If you are 55 or over, you can make a pension contribution and elect for it to start paying out immediately. At its best, an additional-rate taxpayer would make a contribution of £3,600 gross, which would equate to a net contribution after 50 per cent tax relief of £1,800, take a lump sum of £900 (25 per cent of the fund value) and the investment would give a gross pension of about £200 per year every year (depending on age, gender, etc.).

This represents a return of over 15 per cent. Even basic-rate taxpayers would have a return of over ten per cent per annum.

## CHAPTER 4

# For married couples and civil partners

**17.** Equalise your incomes

**18.** Pay your spouse or civil partner to work in your business

**19.** Use the transferable tax allowance for married couples and civil partners

**17 Equalise your incomes**

Husbands and wives and civil partners should always try to equalise their incomes as far as possible so that one spouse/partner is not paying tax at a higher rate than the other. Investments generating interest and dividends can be either moved to joint ownership, or given entirely to the other spouse/partner. Assets that create income (e.g. rented-out land and property) should similarly be put into joint ownership or transferred entirely to the other spouse/partner.

If you are self-employed and your spouse/partner doesn't work, could you employ them in your business? If so, do make sure that you have a contract of employment and that you observe the National Minimum Wage regulations, that what you pay actually changes hands in a demonstrable way and that the pay is commensurate with the services provided.

Alternatively, provided you can show that your spouse/partner plays a significant role in the business you can make them a partner and then the profits can be shared between you.

In other words, where possible, ensure that the spouse/partner with little or no income utilises the personal tax-free allowance, currently £10,600.

 **18 Pay your spouse/civil partner to work in your business**

Where a spouse/partner works in the family business and payment of wages can be justified, it's generally beneficial to pay at least the equivalent of the lower earnings limit (£112 per week for 2015/16) and up to the primary threshold (£155 per week for 2015/16). Not only will this be a tax-deductible expense for the employing spouse/partner, but also it will maintain the employee's National Insurance record for state pension purposes. Assuming there is no other income, there will be no tax or National Insurance Contributions to pay.

Don't forget that you must comply with the National Minimum Wage rates, which are currently (from 1 October 2014) £6.50 per hour for those aged 21 and above, and £5.13 per hour for 18- to 20-year-olds. These rates increase from 1 October 2015 to £6.70 and £5.30 respectively. Plans were announced in the 2015 Summer Budget to significantly increase these rates and change the name to the National Living Wage.

This idea is a useful money saver but you have to do things properly. To make things simpler we are going to imagine that you are a married man running a business, but it could be the other way around or, alternatively, it could involve any business person employing anyone who lives with, or is related to, them and who might reasonably be considered to become an employee.

The way it works is that if you employ your wife for (say) £130 per week, if she has no other earnings or income, she will pay no tax on this pay and you, as her employer, will have reduced your tax bill by more than £1,300. But do watch the following points:

- You need to record the work that she will be doing and the work has to equate to a real contribution to the business. In other words, you cannot just pay her this money without her doing anything in the business at all – HMRC won't allow the payments as a business expense. We include a template of a form (see Appendix page 120) that you both might complete and sign as being evidence that she is genuinely working. You simply keep this document to present to HMRC if they ask for it.

- The payment of her wages has to happen in a demonstrable way, e.g. by bank transfer from the business account into her personal account.

- As we have just said, you need to watch out for the minimum wage. You would not be allowed to pay less than that sum, which usually changes each October.

This mechanism can be taken a step further due to the Employment Allowance. Provided that you are entitled to claim it (which most businesses will be) this allows the first £2,000 of employer's National Insurance to be reclaimed. Therefore, if an employee was taken on and paid £10,600 in the year (and this was their only income) there would be no employer's NI to pay, as it would be covered by the Employment Allowance, the business would reduce its tax liability by £2,120, the employee would pay no Income Tax and would only suffer (approximately) £305 of employee's National Insurance.

## 19 Use the transferable tax allowance for married couples and civil partners

From 6 April 2015, i.e. for the 2015/16 tax year, it is possible under certain circumstances for one spouse/civil partner to transfer to the other spouse/civil partner some of their unused personal allowances.

The transferor can only transfer unused allowances up to a maximum of £1,060 for the year, and the transferee must not be liable to higher rate tax. It is currently possible to register an interest in this with HMRC on their website.

Couples who are eligible for the Married Couples Allowance, which can only be claimed by those born before 6 April 1935, will not be eligible.

# CHAPTER 5
# For employees

20. Claim a flat-rate expense allowance
21. Professional subscriptions
22. Claim incidental expenses when travelling on business
23. Claim expenses against your employment income
24. Claim for the use of your home as an office
25. Submit your Tax Return on time
26. Join the company pension scheme
27. When losing your job
28. Would you pay less tax if you went self-employed?
29. Moving because of your job?
30. Employee-owners

# 20 Claim a flat-rate expense allowance

Certain employees are entitled to a flat-rate expense allowance to cover items such as special clothing, tools, etc. The list below provides details of how much you can claim. You can claim the allowance for the current year and the previous three years.

|  | £ |
|---|---|
| **Agriculture** – All workers | 100 |
| **Aluminium** | |
| Continual casting and process operators | 140 |
| De-dimplers | 140 |
| Driers | 140 |
| Drill punchers | 140 |
| Dross unloaders | 140 |
| Firefighters | 140 |
| Furnace operators and their helpers | 140 |
| Leaders | 140 |
| Mouldmen | 140 |
| Pourers | 140 |
| Remelt department labourers | 140 |
| Roll flatteners | 140 |
| Cable hands | 80 |
| Case makers | 80 |
| Labourers | 80 |
| Mates | 80 |
| Truck drivers and measurers | 80 |
| Storekeepers | 80 |
| Apprentices | 60 |
| All other workers | 120 |
| **Banks** – Uniformed employees | 60 |
| **Brass and copper** – All workers | 120 |
| **Building** | |
| Joiners and carpenters | 140 |
| Cement workers | 80 |
| Roofing felt | 80 |
| Asphalt labourers | 80 |
| Labourers and navvies | 60 |
| All other workers | 120 |
| **Building materials** | |
| Stonemasons | 120 |
| Tile makers and labourers | 60 |
| All other workers | 80 |
| **Clothing** | |
| Lace makers | 60 |

| | |
|---|---|
| Hosiery bleachers | 60 |
| Dyers | 60 |
| Scourers and knitters | 60 |
| Knitwear bleachers and dyers | 60 |
| All other workers | 60 |
| **Constructional engineering** | |
| Blacksmiths and their strikers | 140 |
| Burners | 140 |
| Caulkers | 140 |
| Chippers | 140 |
| Drillers | 140 |
| Erectors | 140 |
| Fitters | 140 |
| Holders-up | 140 |
| Markers-off | 140 |
| Platers | 140 |
| Riggers | 140 |
| Riveters | 140 |
| Rivet heaters | 140 |
| Scaffolders | 140 |
| Sheeters | 140 |
| Template workers | 140 |
| Turners and welders | 140 |
| Banksmen labourers | 80 |
| Shophelpers | 80 |
| Slewers and straighteners | 80 |
| Apprentices and storekeepers | 60 |
| All other workers | 100 |
| **Electrical and electricity supply** | |
| Those workers incurring laundry costs only | 60 |
| All other workers | 120 |
| **Engineering** | |
| Pattern makers | 140 |
| Labourers, supervisory and unskilled workers | 80 |
| Apprentices and storekeepers | 60 |
| Motor mechanics in garage repair shops | 120 |
| All other workers | 120 |

## Fire service

| | |
|---|---|
| Uniformed firefighters and fire officers | 80 |

| | |
|---|---|
| **Food** – All workers | 60 |
| **Forestry** – All workers | 100 |
| **Glass** – All workers | 80 |

## Healthcare

| | |
|---|---|
| Ambulance staff on active service | 140 |
| Nurses | 100 |
| Midwives | 100 |
| Chiropodists | 100 |
| Dental nurses | 100 |
| Occupational, speech and other therapists | 100 |
| Phlebotomists | 100 |
| Physiotherapists | 100 |
| Radiographers | 100 |
| Plaster room orderlies | 100 |
| Hospital porters | 100 |
| Ward clerks | 100 |
| Sterile supply workers | 100 |
| Hospital domestics | 100 |
| Hospital catering staff | 100 |
| Laboratory staff | 60 |
| Pharmacists | 60 |
| Pharmacy assistants | 60 |
| Uniformed ancillary staff | 60 |

## Heating

| | |
|---|---|
| Pipe fitters and plumbers | 120 |
| Coverers | 120 |
| Laggers | 120 |
| Domestic glaziers | 120 |
| Heating engineers and their mates | 120 |
| All other workers | 100 |

## Iron and steel

| | |
|---|---|
| Day labourers | 80 |
| General labourers | 80 |
| Stockmen | 80 |
| Timekeepers | 80 |
| Warehouse staff | 80 |
| Weighmen | 80 |
| Apprentices | 60 |
| All other workers | 140 |

## Iron mining

| | |
|---|---|
| Fillers | 120 |
| Miners | 120 |
| Underground workers | 120 |
| All other workers | 100 |

## Leather

| | |
|---|---|
| Curriers (wet workers) | 80 |
| Fellmongering workers | 80 |
| Tanning operatives (wet) | 80 |
| All other workers | 60 |

## Particular engineering

| | |
|---|---|
| Pattern makers | 140 |
| Chainmakers | 120 |
| Cleaners | 120 |
| Galvanisers | 120 |
| Tinners | 120 |
| Wire drawers in the wire drawing industry | 120 |
| Toolmakers in the lock-making industry | 120 |
| Apprentices and storekeepers | 60 |
| All other workers | 80 |

## Police force

| | |
|---|---|
| Police officers (ranks up to and including Chief Inspector) | 140 |
| Police community safety officers | 140 |

| | |
|---|---|
| **Precious metals** – All workers | 100 |

## Printing – Letter press section using rotary presses

| | |
|---|---|
| Electrical engineers | 140 |
| Electro-typers | 140 |
| Ink and roller markers | 140 |
| Machine minders | 140 |
| Maintenance engineers | 140 |
| Stereotypers | 140 |
| Benchhands | 60 |
| Compositors | 60 |
| Readers | 60 |
| T & E section | 60 |
| Wireroom operators | 60 |
| Warehousemen | 60 |
| All other workers | 100 |

## Prisons

| | |
|---|---|
| Uniformed prison officers (Don't forget to claim for the costs of keeping your dog) | 80 |

## Public service – Dock and inland waterways

| | |
|---|---|
| Dockers | 80 |
| Dredger drivers | 80 |
| Hopper steerers | 80 |
| All other workers | 60 |

## Public transport

| | |
|---|---|
| Garage hands including cleaners | 80 |

| | | | | |
|---|---|---|---|---|
| Conductors and drivers | 60 | **Textiles and textile printing** | | |
| **Quarrying** – All workers | 100 | Carders | | 120 |
| | | Carding engineers | | 120 |
| **Railways** | | Overlookers | | 120 |
| All workers except craftsmen | 100 | Technicians in spinning mills | | 120 |
| (For craftsmen, see appropriate industry) | | All other workers | | 80 |
| | | **Vehicles** | | |
| **Seamen** | | Builders | | 140 |
| Carpenters (passenger liners) | 165 | Railway vehicle repairers | | 140 |
| Carpenters (cargo vessels, | | Railway wagon lifters | | 140 |
| tankers, coasters and ferries) | 140 | Railway vehicle painters and | | |
| | | letterers | | 80 |
| **Shipyards** | | Railway wagon, etc. builders' and | | |
| Blacksmiths and their strikers | 140 | repairers' assistants | | 80 |
| Boilermakers | 140 | All other workers | | 60 |
| Burners | 140 | **Wood and furniture** | | |
| Carpenters | 140 | Carpenters | | 140 |
| Caulkers | 140 | Cabinet makers | | 140 |
| Drillers | 140 | Joiners | | 140 |
| Furnacemen | 140 | Wood carvers | | 140 |
| Holders-up | 140 | Wood cutting machinists | | 140 |
| Fitters | 140 | Artificial limb makers (other than | | |
| Platers | 140 | in wood) | | 120 |
| Plumbers | 140 | Organ builders | | 120 |
| Riveters | 140 | Packaging case makers | | 120 |
| Sheet ironworkers | 140 | Coopers not providing own tools | | 60 |
| Shipwrights | 140 | Labourers | | 60 |
| Tubers | 140 | Polishers | | 60 |
| Welders | 140 | Upholsterers | | 60 |
| Labourers | 80 | All other workers | | 100 |
| Apprentices and storekeepers | 60 | | | |
| All other workers | 100 | | | |

HM Revenue & Customs' (HMRC) website (www.hmrc.gov.uk/manuals/eimanual/index.htm) at Employment Income Manual 50000 to 70199 contains a lot of information about particular occupations and the expenses that can be claimed for them. For example, nursing staff (which includes midwives of all grades, auxiliaries, students and assistants) can claim £100 per annum laundry allowance, £12 per annum shoe allowance and £6 per annum stocking allowance. (For male nurses this can include socks.)

We therefore strongly recommend everyone having a look at this part of the website to ensure that they are claiming their due.

You claim under Box 18 on the employment pages of the Tax Return.

**21 Professional subscriptions**

If you are an employee and you pay professional subscriptions and:

- you are required to do so as a condition of your employment; or
- the activities of the body are directly relevant to your employment;

then provided the professional body is referred to in List 3 (which can be found on HMRC's website at www.hmrc.gov.uk/list3/index.htm), you can claim tax relief for the subscription.

You claim under Box 19 on the employment pages of the Tax Return.

 **22 Claim incidental expenses when travelling on business**

If you are an employee and you have to travel as part of your job, you can claim for your travel costs. This doesn't include ordinary commuting from home to your normal place of work. However, if you work on a site, i.e. you don't have a normal fixed place of work, you can claim the cost of home to site travel provided the duration of your work at the specific site doesn't exceed 24 months.

Incidental personal expenses for items such as newspapers, personal phone calls and laundry incurred while away overnight on business trips are tax free providing the employer pays or reimburses no more than £5 per night for UK trips and £10 for overseas trips. If these limits are exceeded, the whole amount is taxable.

The full cost of meals and accommodation while travelling or staying away on business is also an allowable expense.

You claim under Box 17 on the employment pages of the Tax Return.

Rather than claiming actual travelling costs, if you use your own car for business travel, you can claim for business mileage – see number 37 for more information.

## (23) Claim expenses against your employment income

If you incur extra costs as an employee, keep a record of the details and dates on which the expenditure was incurred, together with the bills, and you may be able to claim it on your Tax Return – see Box 20 on the employment pages of the Tax Return.

Here are some items that you might be able to claim for, unless they are covered by one of HMRC's fixed-rate allowances (see number 19) (i.e. you cannot claim more than once):

- Overalls
- Boots
- Helmets
- Gloves
- Protective clothing
- Necessary equipment
- Tool bag
- Tools
- Trade journals and technical books
- Part of your own telephone bill covering calls to customers
- Gifts to customers paid for by yourself which don't cost more than £50
- Fees or subscriptions to an organisation (professional or otherwise) of which you are a member, although HMRC must approve the organisation
- Journals and publications, etc.

If you have to borrow money to buy equipment that is necessary for your job, then the interest can be claimed as an expense. This doesn't extend to car loans nor to a bank overdraft or credit card interest.

The general rule is that all such expenses must be incurred wholly, exclusively and necessarily for the purposes of the employment.

Elsewhere in this book (see number 19) we cover the fixed allowances you may be able to claim. A number of categories of worker, including healthcare workers, have fixed-rate expenses that they can claim. You may even be able to claim back for earlier years that you haven't already claimed for.

You claim under Box 20 on the employment pages of the Tax Return.

## 24 Claim for the use of your home as an office

If you are required to work at home and use a specific room for this purpose, you can claim an allowance based on a proportion of the total upkeep. You claim under Box 20 on the employment pages of the Tax Return.

Alternatively, you can claim a fixed amount of £4 per week to cover the additional costs of working at home. This is obviously a small figure but doesn't need to be supported by documentary evidence. If you want to claim a higher sum, it must be based on actual costs incurred.

If you want to claim the actual costs incurred, you should add up all the outgoings for your home (mortgage interest, Council Tax, utility bills etc.) and then divide the total by the number of reception rooms and bedrooms in your home (assuming that you use one of these as an office).

## 25 Submit your Tax Return on time

If you are an employee and have been issued with a Tax Return, submit the completed form manually to HMRC by 31 October or online by 31 December. Not only will HMRC calculate your tax liability for you, but if you do owe any tax, it will include it in next year's tax code provided your employment is continuing.

If an underpayment is included in your tax code, and the amount of extra tax you are paying is causing you hardship, ask HMRC to spread the payment over two or three years.

## 26 Join the company pension scheme

If your employer offers access to a pension scheme, it's almost certainly a good thing to do. You might consider opting for a salary sacrifice by directing part of your pay into a pension fund. This will save you tax but the procedure can be somewhat tortuous (the taxman could disallow it for even a minor error on a form) and the arrangement must be permanent, which rules out one-off pension contributions. If you run your own company, you could set up an EPP (Executive Pension Plan) which can be set up for just one director. EPPs are much more flexible than salary sacrifices but they come with hassle as well as the need for the directors not to fall out! You can get an EPP through an independent financial adviser.

## Auto-enrolment

All employers will have to provide workers with a workplace pension scheme by law over the next few years. The biggest employers started doing this in October 2012. This is called automatic enrolment because employees will automatically be enrolled into the scheme unless they choose to opt out. The date by which businesses must start doing this (called a 'staging date') depends on how many people there are on the payroll.

The scheme is being phased in from October 2012 for the largest employers, through to April 2017 for the smallest. New employers from 1 April 2012 will join the scheme between May 2017 and February 2018. The point of the scheme is to have both employer and employee contributing towards the employee's retirement. The amount to be contributed increases over time to a currently proposed maximum of 3 per cent for the employer and 5 per cent for the employee. Both parties will gain tax relief on the pension contributions.

If you are an employer and you don't already offer workers a workplace pension scheme, you must set one up before your business's staging date. If you already have a workplace pension scheme, check if you can use it for automatic enrolment.

You must enrol into the scheme all workers who:

- are aged between 22 and the State Pension age;

- earn at least £10,000 a year;

- work in the UK.

One potential pitfall is that being automatically enrolled in your employer's pension scheme automatically overrides a claim for Fixed Protection for those with pension pots in excess of £1.25m. If you are fortunate enough to be in this position, beware.

## 27  When losing your job

If you lose your job, you may be entitled to a tax-free lump sum of up to £30,000. This will apply if you have been made redundant because your job no longer exists. If you are allowed to keep your company car as part of your redundancy package, the market value of the car will be taken into account in calculating the £30,000. Payments in excess of this amount will be taxable as well as payments made in recognition of past services.

Most other lump-sum/ex gratia payments will be taxable unless made as compensation for the company breaching your contract of employment.

However, if your contract of employment gives you a right to compensation when your employment ends, then the lump sum will be taxable regardless of the amount.

Statutory redundancy payments are not taxable but they do count towards the £30,000 limit.

 ## 28  Would you pay less tax if you went self-employed?

The answer is almost certainly 'yes' because there are many more expenses that you can claim. However, if you are going to go self-employed, you have to do so properly or HMRC will catch up with you and either you or your deemed employer will suffer the tax consequences. HMRC are clamping down on people who claim to be self-employed but are, in reality, employees. There is already specific legislation being introduced aimed at ensuring that partners in limited liability partnerships (LLPs) are genuinely self-employed rather than being employees. There will also be backdated National Insurance Contributions to pay, interest on the late payments and, on top of that, the taxman will demand a penalty. So do make sure that you get it right.

To help you find out whether HMRC is likely to accept that you are truly self-employed, here is a set of questions that should give you an idea:

**1.** Is there a contract of service, i.e. a contract of employment?
   A 'no' answer indicates self-employment.

2. Is there a contract for services, i.e. a notice supplied by the person carrying out the work (A), indicating the nature of goods or services they will provide to B (this need not be written)?

   A 'yes' answer indicates self-employment.

3. Is the person who does the work in business on their own account?

   A 'yes' answer indicates self-employment.

4. If the person is in business on their own account, has evidence been provided that this is indeed the case (e.g. copy accounts, the payment of Class 2 National Insurance Contributions)?

   A 'yes' answer indicates self-employment.

5. Are the hours worked decided by the person doing the work?

   A 'yes' answer indicates self-employment.

6. Are the days worked decided by the person doing the work?

   A 'yes' answer indicates self-employment.

7. Does the person doing the work decide when to take their own holidays?

   A 'yes' answer indicates self-employment.

8. Does the business proprietor supervise the work?

   A 'no' answer indicates self-employment.

9. Is the person part and parcel of the business?

   A 'no' answer indicates self-employment.

10. Does the person supply tools and/or materials when they carry out the work?

    A 'yes' answer indicates self-employment.

11. Does the person doing the work give the business an invoice for the work done?

    A 'yes' answer indicates self-employment.

12. Does the business calculate how much to pay the person doing the work and give a payslip?

    A 'no' answer indicates self-employment.

13. Is self-employment the intention of both parties?

    A 'yes' answer indicates self-employment.

14. Is the person bound by the customer care credo of the business?

A 'no' answer indicates self-employment.

**15.** Is the person carrying out the work required to wear a uniform or dress tidily at the diktat of the business?

A 'no' answer indicates self-employment.

**16.** Is the person carrying out the work provided with a car or transport by the business?

A 'no' answer indicates self-employment.

**17.** In the event of sickness, does the business continue to pay the person while not at work?

A 'no' answer indicates self-employment.

**18.** Is the person carrying out the work at liberty to work for other businesses?

A 'yes' answer indicates self-employment.

**19.** Is the person carrying out the work required to work in order to perform a specific task?

A 'yes' answer indicates self-employment.

**20.** Does the business, on asking this person to carry out work for it, assume any responsibility or liability characteristic of an employment, such as employment protection, employees' liability, pension entitlements, etc.?

A 'no' answer indicates self-employment.

**21.** Is the person who does the work paid an agreed price per job?

A 'yes' answer indicates self-employment (i.e. they are not paid for the hours they work but for the work carried out).

**22.** Is the work carried out regularly?

A 'no' answer indicates self-employment.

**23.** Does the individual work for other people?

A 'yes' answer indicates self-employment.

**24.** Does the person carrying out the work advertise?

A 'yes' answer indicates self-employment.

**25.** Does the person carrying out the work have headed stationery?

A 'yes' answer indicates self-employment.

**26.** Can the person send a substitute? If so, has this ever happened?

A 'yes' answer indicates self-employment.

**27.** Does the person have to rectify faulty workmanship in their own time and at their own expense?

A 'yes' answer indicates self-employment.

 ## 29 Moving because of your job?

If you are moving home because of your job, qualifying removal expenses and benefits are exempt from Income Tax. The maximum tax-free amount is £8,000 per move provided that expenses and benefits are incurred in the period from the date of the job change up to the end of the tax year following the one in which the move occurred.

This applies whether it's a new job with a new employer, a new job with an existing employer or you are continuing your current job but at a new location. Issues of ease of daily travelling from the old and new homes have to be regarded and the expenses have to be reimbursed by your employer. Most of the costs reasonably related to the move, subject to limits, are allowed.

The favourable tax and National Insurance Contributions treatment of these payments should make them attractive to employee and employer alike when considering relocation packages.

 ## 30 Employee-owners

This is a new employee status created by the government. With effect from 1 September 2013, these employees have fewer employee rights than normal employees. As compensation, they must receive at least £2,000 of shares in the company that they work for (or its parent company). The first £2,000 of shares received are free of an Income Tax and National Insurance charge. Furthermore, capital gains of up to £50,000 on the disposal of the shares will be exempt from Capital Gains Tax. Because this particular arrangement involves sacrificing some normal employment rights, it should be entered into with care, and preferably after taking professional advice on the implications.

This employee shareholder status should not be confused with a normal employee who own shares in their employer, e.g. someone who happens to work for Tesco owning Tesco plc shares.

## CHAPTER 6
# For employers

# 31 Short-term employment contracts

If you are an employer, particularly where your business' workload varies significantly throughout the year, do consider having your employees on short-term contracts. This gives you flexibility if you need to reduce the number of staff and avoids your having to make redundancy payments. You are still at liberty to give fresh contracts to those people whose services you wish to retain.

# 32 Share schemes

Offer your employees shares under one of the many share schemes available. This can be a tax-efficient way of passing a valuable benefit to an employee. What are the different schemes and rules for providing shares for employees?

## Share Incentive Plan

A Share Incentive Plan (SIP) is a plan established by a company and approved by HM Revenue & Customs (HMRC). Employees may allocate part of their salary to shares in the company ('partnership shares') without paying tax or National Insurance Contributions, nor are employers' National Insurance Contributions payable. Employers may also give free shares to employees, including extra free shares for employees who have partnership shares ('matching shares'), and the cost of the shares and of running the scheme are tax-deductible. The maximum you can allocate as an employer is £1,800 per year for partnership shares and £3,600 per year for free shares, although employers may set lower limits. Note: all types of share issued to employees must be reported to HMRC on Form 42 ('Employment-related securities') within 30 days; failure to so do will entail a fine of £300 per employee.

If the employee takes shares out of the scheme within five years, there will be a tax charge. If the shares remain in the scheme for five years or more, they are free of tax and National Insurance Contributions when they are withdrawn.

## Save As You Earn (SAYE) option schemes

Under an approved SAYE scheme, contributions of between £5 and £500 per month are paid by the employee under an SAYE contract with a building society or bank. The option to purchase shares using the SAYE funds can normally be exercised after three, five or seven years when the contract ends. No charge to Income Tax arises on the difference between cost and market value when a share option is exercised, nor at the time that it's granted.

The scheme enables an option to be granted now to acquire shares at today's price. The price at which the option may be exercised must not normally be less than 80 per cent of the market value of the shares at the time the option is granted.

## Company Share Option Plans (CSOPs)

Under a CSOP, the option must not be granted at a discount and the total market value of shares that may be acquired must not exceed £30,000. If these conditions are complied with, there is no tax charge when options are granted. Nor is there a tax charge when the option is exercised, providing options are exercised between three and ten years after they are granted, and not more frequently than once in three years.

The costs of running the scheme are tax-deductible.

## Enterprise Management Incentive (EMI)

Companies with gross assets not exceeding £30 million can grant tax and National-Insurance-contribution-advantaged share options worth up to £250,000 to any number of employees, subject to a total value of £3 million.

## Schemes outside the HMRC-approved range of schemes

These will suffer tax and National Insurance Contributions.

Needless to say, professional advice must be sought.

## (33) Tax-free benefits you can give to employees

Give your employees tax-free benefits, such as:

- a canteen if it's available to everybody;
- car and bike parking at work;
- childcare costs and vouchers – not taxable up to £55 per week;
- computers provided solely for business use; if any private use is not significant, they are exempt from a benefit charge;
- exam prizes – they are not taxable if they are reasonable and not part of the employment contract;
- eye tests and corrective glasses;
- mileage allowances (up to 45p per mile for the first 10,000 miles and 25p per mile after that);
- mobile telephones;
- nurseries and play schemes run by the employer;
- outplacement counselling;
- pension contributions and death-in-service cover;
- relocation expenses – tax free up to £8,000;
- retraining and counselling on leaving employment;
- share incentive schemes – not taxable if approved by HMRC;
- travel to work on a works' bus;
- workplace sports facilities;
- suggestion scheme awards;
- medical check-ups for employees and their families;
- bicycles provided for employees as long as they are used for travel between home and work and private use is limited (this includes bicycle safety equipment);

- Christmas parties open to all staff. You can now spend up to £150 per head. It will be a tax-deductible business expense and tax free for your employees.

The benefit to the employer is that the employees get a good deal, while the employer gets tax relief on the expenditure incurred.

##  34 Tax-free loans to employees

An employer can make an interest-free loan to an employee of up to £10,000 in the tax year, without there being any tax or National Insurance charge. This could be used to cover the cost of purchasing a season ticket for travelling to work, for instance.

## Tax free loans to employees

# CHAPTER 7
# Company vehicles

## (35) Vans have some tax-saving attractions

If you ,as an employee, are provided with a company van and you use the van for private purposes, you pay tax on a standard benefit of £3,150 per year, regardless of the age of the van. If the van is shared, then the taxable benefit is spread between the sharers.

However, if the van is made available to you mainly for business travel and the terms on which it is made available prohibit its private use other than for ordinary commuting from your home to your place of work, then the taxable benefit is nil. Insignificant private use is disregarded; HMRC have obligingly provided some guidance on what they think this means:

Examples of insignificant use are when an employee (using the van):

- takes an old mattress or other rubbish to the tip once or twice a year;

- regularly makes a slight detour to stop at a newsagent on the way to work;

- calls at the dentist on his way home.

Examples of use which are not insignificant are when an employee:

- uses the van to do the supermarket shopping every week;

- takes the van away on a week's holiday;

- uses the van outside of work for social activities.

There is also a fuel benefit charge of £594. This does not apply if the fuel is made available for business travel only or the employee is required to pay for the fuel used for private purposes and does, in fact, do so.

Electric vans do not currently attract a benefit charge.

## (36) Company cars

The company car tax charge is calculated by referring to:

- the list price of the car when new, plus any additional items fitted and less any capital contributions made by the employee; and

## Car benefit charges based on CO$_2$ emissions

| CO$_2$ emissions in grams per kilometre | Tax is based on the following percentage of the price of the car* | |
| --- | --- | --- |
| **2015/16** | **%** | |
| 0-94 | 13 | |
| 95-99 | 14 | |
| 100-104 | 15 | |
| 105-109 | 16 | |
| 110-114 | 17 | |
| 115-119 | 18 | |
| 120-124 | 19 | |
| 125-129 | 20 | |
| 130-134 | 21 | |
| 135-139 | 22 | |
| 140-144 | 23 | * Diesels pay a 3% |
| 145-149 | 24 | surcharge on all |
| 150-154 | 25 | engine sizes, |
| 155-159 | 26 | with a maximum |
| 160-164 | 27 | payable of 37% |
| 165-169 | 28 | |
| 170-174 | 29 | |
| 175-179 | 30 | |
| 180-184 | 31 | |
| 185-189 | 32 | |
| 190-194 | 33 | |
| 195-199 | 34 | |
| 200-204 | 35 | |
| 205-209 | 36 | |
| More than 210 | 37 | |

- the CO$_2$ emissions (which are shown on the V5 vehicle registration document) for cars registered on or after 1 March 2001 (see the table above). Emission levels can also be found on the internet at the Vehicle Certification Agency's website (www.vca.gov.uk) and that of the Society of Motor Manufacturers and Traders Limited (www.smmt.co.uk).

It is the $CO_2$ emissions which determine the percentage by which the adjusted list price is multiplied to give the taxable benefit. Diesel cars are subject to a three per cent surcharge.

If a vehicle isn't available for the full year, then the charge is reduced pro rata.

Therefore, selecting a car with lower emissions and/or a lower list price will reduce your tax liability.

Electric cars do not currently attract a benefit charge.

If you are self-employed and are going to use a car for business purposes, you can claim Enhanced Capital Allowances (see number 46) if your new car has emissions not exceeding 94g/km. You will be able to claim 100 per cent First-Year Allowances (subject to an adjustment for any private use).

This also applies to companies buying company cars.

Companies should also consider the cost effectiveness of leasing vehicles for their employees as the recent changes to the capital allowances legislation have made car purchases less attractive for cars emitting more than 130g/km.

Anyone buying a new car pays a different rate of Vehicle Excise Duty for the first year, before reverting to the normal scale for the second and subsequent years

### Graduated Vehicle Excise Duty for 2015/2016 for private vehicles (registered since March 2001)

**First-year-rates**

| Band | CO₂ (g/km) | Rate (£) |
|------|-----------|----------|
| A | Up to 100 | 0 |
| B | 101–110 | 0 |
| C | 111–120 | 0 |
| D | 121–130 | 0 |
| E | 131–140 | 130 |
| F | 141–150 | 145 |
| G | 151–165 | 180 |
| H | 166–175 | 295 |

| I | 176–185 | 350 |
| J | 186–200 | 490 |
| K | 201–225 | 640 |
| L | 226–255 | 870 |
| M | 256 and over | 1,100 |

**Standard rates for cars already registered**

| Band | CO$_2$ (g/km) | Rate (£) |
| --- | --- | --- |
| A | Up to 100 | 0 |
| B | 101–110 | 20 |
| C | 111–120 | 30 |
| D | 121–130 | 110 |
| E | 131–140 | 130 |
| F | 141–150 | 145 |
| G | 151–165 | 180 |
| H | 166–175 | 205 |
| I | 176–185 | 225 |
| J | 186–200 | 265 |
| K | 201–225 | 290 |
| L | 226–255 | 490 |
| M | 256 and over | 505 |

#  The best (and worst) ways of providing company cars

The rules for taxation of company cars now place a much greater emphasis on CO$_2$ emissions. You might find the following alternative scenarios interesting to say the least.

If a business owner, or company director, wants to buy a new company car, which will be used extensively in their business, but privately as well, they might consider two options which have **very** different effects for tax purposes. They might buy a new car costing £42,000 and emitting 287g/km. They might even find that the dealer offers a £10,000 discount (to help boost sales in slow times). So far so good. However, the tax payable by the director personally (assuming that they pay tax at 40 per cent) for the provision of this car (based on £42,000 as the discount is ignored) is £6,216 annually but the tax relief gained by the company (assuming that it pays Corporation Tax at 20 per cent) for buying it (based on what it actually pays – £32,000) is only £512 in the first year, and less than that every year thereafter. So you see there is a net tax cost of over £5,000 for every year the company owns this car. There is also the company's liability to Class 1A National Insurance Contributions at 13.8 per cent on the benefit figure of £5,216, which is nearly £720.

Before we get to the better options, what if, instead of buying the car, the company were to lease it? In this case, the company would be able to claim 85 per cent of the costs of leasing; so this might well be worth considering, instead of an outright purchase, but the tax charge on the director, personally, is still penal.

On the other hand, if the director were to own the car, and if the company were to pay them a dividend of £32,000 to buy the car, the only tax that anyone would pay would be a one-off charge payable to the director of £8,000 on the dividend (assuming they pay tax at 40 per cent).

Having said this, if you want to go for a cheaper option, there are still cases where it's not that disadvantageous for the company to own the car. In stark contrast to the above, if the car (say a diesel) were to cost £12,500 and emit less than 75g/km, not only can the company get a 100 per cent First-Year Allowance (tax saving £2,500); but also, the tax payable by the director would be only £800 per annum (assuming they pay tax at 40 per cent). A lot less than the person buying the gas guzzler.

In short, what matters now is the rate of emissions of the car you intend to buy, as well as how you buy it.

We also hear that some owners/directors are buying low-emitting cars (as in our second example) to provide to their children. All costs are then deductible in the company (including the (large) insurance premiums) and the director pays tax as noted above (£800 per annum in our example).

If you reimburse your employer for the costs of private motoring in order to avoid a scale charge, it is now absolutely vital that reimbursement must be made in the tax year in which the private use was undertaken

## 38 Claim approved mileage allowance payments for your car

If you are an employee and you use your own car for business purposes you can claim back 45p per mile from your employer for the first 10,000 business miles in a tax year and 25p per mile thereafter. If your employer reimburses less than the mileage figure, you can claim the difference in your Tax Return (Box 17 on the employment pages). If you can persuade your employer to pay you an extra 5p per mile for carrying a business passenger, it would also be tax free, but you can't claim it if your employer doesn't pay you for it. If you use a motorbike, you can claim 24p for business mileage and if you use a bicycle, you can claim 20p.

 ## 39 Avoid the fuel tax charge

If your employer pays for all your fuel but you repay them for all your private fuel and if you keep a careful and detailed record of every car journey undertaken whether business or private, then you don't have to pay tax on the fuel provided for business purposes. However, you have to bear in mind that travel from home to the place of work is considered to be commuting and therefore, private mileage.

The company car fuel multiplier is £22,100. You multiply this by the appropriate percentage taken from the table on page 43 to work out the taxable benefit for your car. It is our view that there must be very few instances where it is beneficial for you to be provided with fuel for private motoring by your employer.

 ## 40 Own your own car rather than using your employer's

The tax payable on car benefits is now so high that it can often be cheaper to own your own car and use it for your employer's business. You would need to work it out and we certainly know of cases where, while the tax is high, the employee would rather suffer the tax than have to pay for all the outgoings that having one's own car entails. However, as we say, with the tax being high, it's quite likely that you would be better off if you owned your own car rather than pay the taxes that driving an employer's business car attracts.

# CHAPTER 8

# For those running their own business

## 41 Travelling expenses

| Expenses | Employer | Self-employed | Can VAT (input tax) be reclaimed? |
|---|---|---|---|
| | Where expenses are incurred by the employer, whether a self-employed trader, a partnership or a company | Where a self-employed trader incurs these expenses on their own behalf | |
| Entertaining own staff | Allowable | Allowable | Yes* |
| Business travel between place of business and customers, etc. (but not home) | Allowable | Allowable | Yes |
| Hotel bills, etc. | Allowable | Allowable | Yes, so long as it's billed to the VAT-registered trader |
| *Drinks and meals away from home:* | | | |
| 1. Working/selling | Allowable | Not allowable | Yes* |
| 2. On training course | Allowable | Allowable | Yes* |
| 3. Buying, etc. trips | Allowable | Allowable | Yes* |
| *Entertaining business clients:* | Not allowable | Not allowable | No |
| Car parking | Allowable | Allowable | Yes |
| Trade show expenses | Allowable | Allowable | Yes |
| Petrol | Allowable | Allowable – business proportion only | Yes** |

*But not if there is any measurable degree of business entertainment.

**But if the input VAT is reclaimed, remember to include the scale charge in your output tax on the VAT Return.

 ## 42 Limited companies

As a private individual, the higher rates of Income Tax are 40 per cent and 45 per cent and that starts when your taxable income (i.e. income after any personal allowances which are available) reaches £31,765 and £150,000 respectively. On top of the Income Tax bill, there is Class 4 National Insurance to add, at nine per cent up of income between £8,060 and £42,385, and then two per cent thereafter.

However, for a company, the highest rate of Corporation Tax is 20 per cent

If you and your spouse have a business and the taxable profits are £100,000, if we ignore personal allowances, here is how the sums work out:

| Self-employment/partnership | | | | Tax, etc. payable |
|---|---|---|---|---|
| Profits £100,000 | | | | |
| | | *Husband* | *Wife* | |
| *Profits shared* | | £50,000 | £50,000 | |
| Income Tax | | | | |
| 31,765 | 20% | 6,353 | 6,353 | |
| 18,235 | 40% | 7,294 | 7,294 | |
| 50,000 | | 13,647 | 13,647 | 27,294 |
| Class 4 National Insurance | | | | |
| 8,060 | 0% | 0 | 0 | |
| 34,325 | 9% | 3,089 | 3,089 | |
| 7,615 | 2% | 152 | 152 | |
| 50,000 | | 3,241 | 3,241 | 6,482 |
| Total tax and National Insurance payable | | | | £33,776 |
| **The money the Chancellor allows you to keep** | | | | **£66,224**    66% |
| Company profits £100,000 | Corporation Tax 20% | | | 20,000 |
| **The money the Chancellor allows the company to keep** | | | | **£80,000**    80% |

In other words, the tax saved by trading through a limited company appears to be over £13,000.

However, it's not quite as simple as that (it never is!) because if you have paid yourself a salary from the company, then you may have suffered the higher personal rates of tax, and the company and you may both have suffered National Insurance Contributions. On the other hand and in addition, you may have paid yourself a dividend, which can be a tax efficient way of withdrawing cash from the company. You can also control the amount of income you receive to avoid higher-rate tax.

So it's all quite complicated and professional advice must be sought. But if these figures relate in any way to what you are doing, you should discuss this with your accountant – there could be a large tax saving to be made.

Given that the personal allowance is reduced by £1 for every £2 of income over £100,000, it is more important than ever that, where possible, income levels are controlled carefully.

For those who wish to get the best possible tax position from running a limited company, here is a simplified formula to help directors /shareholders enjoy a tax-free income from their company. This formula does not mean that the company itself will not have paid any tax, because it almost certainly will have done so. The key is to ensure that the director/shareholder does not have a gross income in 2015/16 from all sources of more than £42,385. If this is the case, and if he or she pays themselves a salary of (say) £7,500, then, if the net dividend they pay themselves is no more than £31,396, they should have no personal tax or National Insurance to pay, nor will the company pay any employer's NIC. As indicated on page 21, taking advantage of the Employment Allowance can increase the tax saving even though a modest amount of employee's National Insurance is paid.

##  43 Don't automatically reclaim VAT on fuel

It's not always a good idea for the self-employed to claim input tax (i.e. the VAT you have to pay) on the fuel used in their car.

The rule over claiming input tax on your fuel purchases is that if you claim VAT on your fuel purchases and some of the fuel is used for private journeys, you have to add the fuel scale charge to your output tax (i.e. the VAT you charge your customers) – you will find the figures for the quarterly fuel scale charge in the Appendix. What this can mean (and is the usual case) is that you can end up paying HM Revenue & Customs (HMRC) more than you are claiming back from it and so this may not be worth your while. The only person who can work out whether it's worth your while is you. The fuel scale charge is based on the $CO_2$ emissions of the car.

##  44 The flat-rate VAT scheme

Are you registered for VAT but hate the complexity of VAT returns? Provided your turnover is less than £150,000 per annum, then it's possible to request that the flat-rate scheme applies. The payment due to HMRC is a percentage of your standard-rated turnover, so you don't have to calculate your input VAT every quarter. The exact percentage applied is determined by the nature of your business activity and full details are available on the HMRC website. Switching to this scheme could save you time and money, but you would have to look at each case on its own merits. If you usually have a large amount of input VAT, then the scheme may not be suitable for you. The rates are periodically revised to include new sectors, as well as increase the amount payable in certain sectors. You should check that the scheme still suits you. There is a one per cent discount for one year for businesses that adopt the flat-rate scheme within one year of registering for VAT.

##  45 National Insurance

While most of the ideas for reducing your tax bill in this book involve larger sums of tax saving, this one concerns one of the smallest figures of savings on offer, if not the smallest.

If you are just starting out in business and in your first year of trading, you are unlikely to make large profits. This is not guaranteed to happen but it usually turns out this way.

Now you have to register your business with HMRC and it will demand that, as a self-employed person, you pay Class 2 National Insurance Contributions of £2.70 per week. Such a sum is unlikely to break the bank but you can get into trouble if you don't pay it.

From 6 April 2015, instead of paying Class 2 NIC contributions monthly, quarterly or 6 monthly, they will be included in with the self-assessment Income Tax and Class 4 NIC liabilities and paid in January and July the following year.

However, if your profits are likely to be under £5,965, you can claim exemption from paying it. Do remember that opting out may affect your entitlement to state pension, Statutory Maternity Pay, Incapacity Benefit, Bereavement Allowance and other contributory benefits. The current rate is only £2.80 per week, which we think is a small price to pay for maintaining your National Insurance Contributions record.

## 46 Annual Investment Allowance and First-Year Allowances

**Annual Investment Allowance:** Expenditure of up to £500,000 per annum (in the period 1 April 2014 to 31 December 2015) on plant, machinery, long-life assets and integral features is relieved **in full** against profits. From 1 January 2016, this allowance is reduced to £200,000. Any expenditure above this limit is relieved using the normal capital allowance rules. The allowance is based on income tax years and so care should be taken when planning large purchases in an accounting period which spans a tax year end date or the date of the decrease.

Where the written down value of the plant and machinery pool is £1,000 or less, this can be written off in full if desired. As a result many small businesses – especially those which are labour rather than capital intensive, as are many service businesses – can claim 100 per cent of their capital expenditure in the year in which they make it.

**Long-life assets:** Long-life assets are items of plant or machinery which are expected to last at least 25 years. The writing down allowance for them is eight per cent. A new 'pool' is created to include long-life assets and integral features. Integral features include electrical systems, cold water systems, heating systems, air conditioning, lifts and escalators.

**First-Year Allowances:** A business can claim 100 per cent First-Year Allowances (i.e. you can effectively write off all the capital costs against your trading profit) if it incurs qualifying expenditure on designated energy-saving or water-saving plant and machinery, cars with very low $CO_2$ emissions less than 95g/km, and goods vehicles withe zero carbon emissions. There is a number of equipment categories, including such things as lighting, heating (combined heat and power, solar thermal systems, heat pumps, boilers, warm air heaters, hand driers), refrigeration, motors and drives, pipework insulation, ventilation and air conditioning equipment, automatic monitoring equipment and uninterruptible power supplies.

If you are considering purchasing plant or equipment that is in the specified categories, then to buy the energy efficient option will (a) give you full tax relief immediately, (b) probably reduce your long-term running costs and (c) help save the planet.

Before spending your money in excess of the current Annual Investment Allowance threshold, find out more about the Enhanced Capital Allowances scheme at https://etl.decc.gov.uk. This list is constantly being updated, so do check it regularly. Purchases relieved under the First Year Allowance heading do not use up any of the Annual Investment Allowance.

 ## 47 The benefit of short-life assets

Items of plant and equipment that have a short life (typically four years or less) should be placed in a short-life assets pool. This will allow a balancing allowance or charge to arise if the asset is disposed of within four years. An election for this to apply to items purchased has to be made within one year after 31 January following the tax year in which the period of accounts ends in which the purchase was made. This relief will only be of benefit if your expenditure on plant and equipment exceeds £250,000 in the year. (See the notes above about the Annual Investment Allowance.)

Failure to make an election (which is irrevocable) will mean that the balancing adjustment for the disposal will only be made when the business ceases.

 ## 48 Use your business's losses

If you have made a trading loss in your business, look carefully at how best it can be utilised. Trading losses can be set against your general taxable income for the year in which they arise and/or the previous year. Also, the losses can be carried forward to set against future profits of the same trade.

In a new business the losses may also be carried back and set against general taxable income of the previous three years, the earliest first.

A loss on cessation can be relieved against trading income of the final year and/or against trading income of the three previous years, latest first.

Ensure that you get relief not only against tax for the losses, but also against your Class 4 National Insurance Contributions liability.

A loss claim can be extended to include relief against capital gains in the year of the loss and/or the previous year.

For individuals carrying on a trade in a non-active capacity, i.e. spending on average less than ten hours per week on commercial activities of the trade, there is an annual limit of £25,000 for losses which can be set against other income in the year, carried back to the previous year or set off against capital gains.

Loss-relief claims can be quite complex, particularly if there are multiple claims. It's vital that the implications of the claims are carefully reviewed and, if necessary, professional advice taken.

HMRC have announced changes to restrict the amount of Income Tax relief that an individual may claim for deduction from their total income in a tax year. The limit applies from the 2013/14 tax year onwards and is the greater of £50,000 or 25 per cent of the individual's adjusted total income.

Reliefs subject to the limit include:

- Trade loss relief against total income
- Early trade losses relief
- Post-cessation trade relief

The limit does not apply to a relief in the following circumstances:

- To deductions of trade loss relief, or post-cessation trade relief, made from profits of the same trade.
- To the extent that the trade loss relief is attributable to deductions of overlap relief.

##  Have you claimed for all your business expenses?

See the template on the following page. The general rule is that all such expenses must be incurred wholly and exclusively for the purposes of the business.

# 50 Farmers and averaging

Farmers and market gardeners, whether trading on their own or in partnership, may average their profits over two tax years if the profit of one year is less than 70 per cent of the profit of the other year. If the profit is between 70 per cent and 75 per cent relative to the other, then there is a marginal relief available. The two-year time limit is being increased to 5 years with effect from 6 April 2016.

The purpose of this treatment is to smooth out the peaks and troughs of good and bad years. You could, for instance, be paying higher-rate tax in one year and nothing in the following year. An averaging claim, while a little complex, can be very worthwhile, as it optimises the use of personal allowances and capital allowances. This not only minimises your tax liabilities, but also it can maximise your entitlements to tax credits and the like.

An averaging claim must be made within a year of 31 January following the end of the second tax year, and a claim cannot be made in the first or last year of trading. The averaging can continue year after year.

# 51 Partnerships

Have a proper partnership deed to prove the partnership exists and make sure there is a partnership bank account and proper letterhead for the same reason.

Partnerships can be tricky things – they are not to be entered into lightly. For one, if your partner goes bust, you could easily find that you are (what is called) 'jointly and severally liable' for his or hers debts. So be very careful whom you go into partnership with.

Partnerships cannot just be set up on a whim. They need to be planned and created properly, and then they may be able to save a significant sum in tax.

What are the golden rules of partnerships and what are the things you should look out for?

The taxman may need proof that what you have created is indeed a partnership. To do this, you should be able to show him:

* a partnership bank account (with the names of the partners or at least

## A template to help you prepare your figures for the self-employed part of the Tax Return

Your name _____ Accounting year end _____

### Self-employment and partnerships

**Sales income**                                                            A

*less*          **Costs of sales,** e.g. raw materials and stocks

      **Construction industry subcontractors' costs**

      **Other direct costs,** e.g. packing and despatch

          **Total cost of sales**                          B

          **Gross profit or loss** A – B                     C

          **Other income**                               D

**Expenditure**

**Employee costs**
Salaries, wages, bonuses, employer's NIC, pension contributions, casual wages, canteen costs, recruitment agency fees, subcontractors' (unless shown above) and other wages costs

**Premises costs**
Rent, ground rent, rates, water, refuse, light and heat, property insurance, security and use of home

**Repairs**
Repair of property, replacements, renewals, maintenance

**General administrative expenses**
Telephone, fax, mobile telephone, stationery, photocopying, printing, postage, courier and computer costs, subscriptions, insurance

**Motoring expenses**
Petrol, servicing, licence, repairs, motor insurance, hire and leasing, car parking, RAC/AA membership

**Travel and subsistence**
Rail, air, bus, etc., travel, taxis, subsistence and hotel costs

**Entertainment**
Staff entertaining (e.g. Christmas party), customer gifts up to £50 per person advertising your business

**Advertising and promotion**
Advertising, promotion, mailshots, free samples, brochures, newsletters, trade shows, etc.

**Legal and professional costs**
Accountancy, legal, architects', surveyors', stocktakers' fees, indemnity insurance

**Bad debts** (if already included in A above)

**Interest**
on bank loans, overdraft and other loans

**Other finance charges**
Bank charges, HP interest, credit card charges, leasing not already included

**Depreciation and losses on sale** (please ask for advice)

**Other items** – please describe

          **Grand total of expenses**                       E

          **Net profit (or loss)** C + D – E

the name of the partnership on the statements);

- letterheads, invoices, business cards, etc;

- advertisements (as in Yellow Pages) in the name of the partnership;

- brochures, if you have them; and

- a proper partnership deed. You really should have one of these, not just to show the taxman, but as a formal record of the terms under which you and your partner(s) agreed to go into business. If something were to go wrong (and partnerships have a habit of going wrong – partners fall out or, worse still, partners can die), it's vital to have recorded what the partners should do in such an eventuality.

## 52 Claiming tax relief on interest

If you borrow money to buy shares in a private company or a share in a partnership, or to buy plant and machinery for business use, you should be able to get tax relief on the interest at your top rate of tax. Similarly, if you borrow money to lend to a partnership of which you are a partner or company in which you are a shareholder, tax relief will be due providing you are not a limited partner or a partner in an investment limited liability partnership (i.e. a business that makes investments). If the loan is to a company, you must own at least five per cent of the issued share capital and also work there, more or less full time, in a managerial capacity for relief to be due.

# CHAPTER 9
# National Insurance

## 53 Get a state pension forecast well before retirement age

If you don't qualify for the full amount, you may be able to boost your entitlement by making additional contributions for earlier years or voluntary contributions for coming years prior to retirement. The forecast can be obtained by filling out Form BR19, by phoning 0845 3000 168, or by making an online application at www.gov.uk/state-pension-statement.

## 54 Don't pay too much National Insurance

If you are employed as well as self-employed, you may be paying too much National Insurance. Consider deferring Class 2 and/or Class 4 contributions and HM Revenue & Customs (HMRC) will then check the position after the end of the tax year. The way Class 2 contributions are being collected changes from 6 April 2015 – see previous chapter – and it has been announced in the Budget that there will be a review of the future of Class 4 NIC, as well as the abolition of Class 2 contributions, in the next Parliament.

Also if you have two or more simultaneous employments, you will pay full Class 1 contributions at each. As a consequence, you might end up paying too much over the course of a complete tax year. In this situation it would be wise to look into applying for a deferment of National Insurance.

Also, when you reach state pension age, you are no longer liable to pay Class 1 or Class 2 National Insurance. The self-employed still have to pay Class 4 National Insurance on their profits up to the end of the tax year in which they become entitled to their state pension.

## 55 Deferral of your state pension

Whether you have yet to start receiving your state pension or are already receiving it, it is possible to defer payment. This can be advantageous if you reach pension age but are continuing to work. It may be that claiming your pension would make you liable to higher rates of tax, for example.

If receipt of your pension is deferred, you can gain an increase in your pension of one per cent for every five weeks of deferral.

If you put off claiming your pension for at least 12 continuous months, you can choose to receive your pension at the normal rate plus a one-off lump sum. This lump sum is taxable, but you may be able to have it paid in a year when you are liable to lower rates of tax than if you had not deferred it.

As you are forgoing your pension now for additional pension later, there is a strong investment aspect to the decision. It is therefore recommended that you take advice on the matter from an independent financial adviser.

##  56 Winter fuel payments

If you were born on or before 5 July 1952, then you will be eligible for winter fuel payments in the winter of 2015 to 2016. This is usually paid automatically to those people who are in receipt of their state pension. However, if you have deferred claiming your state pension, or if you have reached state pension age but do not have any entitlement to a state pension due to insufficient contributions, you can still claim the winter fuel payment. Claims can only be made after 31 March 2015 and you should look at the claims procedure at www.gov.uk/winter-fuel-payments/how-to-claim.

Once you have made a successful claim, subsequent years' payments should be made automatically.

##  57 Topping up your pension entitlement

From 1 October 2015, pensioners who will not be eligible for the new single tier pension will be able to purchase an additional pension by paying Class 3A National Insurance contributions. However, it is only available for those who reach state pension age by 5 April 2016.

The cost will vary according to an individual's age, so independent financial advice should be sought on the matter.

## CHAPTER 10
# Capital Gains Tax

## Make use of the annual Capital Gains Tax exemption (1)

In 2015/16, the Capital Gains Tax annual exemption is £11,100. If you can structure your financial affairs to give you gains each year that don't exceed this figure, you effectively have extra tax-free income. Investments giving rise to gains are most frequently unit trusts and shares, although those held in ISAs and investments in government gilts don't have any capital gains liability.

While most people accept that investments of this type can go down as well as up, if you make investments through an independent financial adviser and you suffer a loss because of poor advice, poor investment management or the adviser going out of business, there is a Financial Services Compensation Scheme, which can pay compensation of up to £50,000 – for more information, visit its website at www.fscs.org.uk.

## Make use of the annual Capital Gains Tax exemption (2)

If there will be tax to pay, consider transferring the asset to the non-tax-paying spouse or civil partner. Assets transferred between spouses and civil partners are exempt and each is entitled to the annual exempt amount of £11,100. The person receiving the asset is deemed to have acquired it at the original cost.

There should be no strings attached to the gift whatsoever, particularly something which might result in the eventual proceeds going back to the transferor. Do be aware however that the inter-spousal/civil partner exemption ends in the year of separation; making transfers of assets in the following tax year could lead to capital gains being crystallised.

## Don't overlook claiming relief for shares that are now worthless

If you have tax to pay, check to see if you have shares in companies that are now worthless. If you do, whatever those shares cost will equal a loss which can be offset against gains. If the shares were new shares issued by the company when you bought them, you may also be able to offset the loss against your taxable income.

 ## 61 Entrepreneurs' Relief

If you sell your business, you may be entitled to Entrepreneurs' Relief, whereby Capital Gains Tax of only ten per cent is charged. This gives preferential treatment to the disposal of business assets. This includes trading businesses either carried on alone or in partnership, assets of that business, shares in the individual's own trading company and assets owned by the individual but used in their trading company or business.

There is a lifetime limit of £10 million upon which the Entrepreneurs' Relief can be claimed, and claims can be made on more than one occasion to utilise the lifetime limit. The business must have been owned for at least one year ending on the date of the disposal. If there is a property involved, i.e. the business was run from a freehold property, then you must sell it within three years of cessation of trading to get the relief.

Furnished holiday letting properties are also regarded as business assets, but not properties used for any other type of letting. To qualify as furnished holiday letting, the property must be:

- available as holiday accommodation for at least 210 days in a tax year; and

- let on a commercial basis for at least 105 days; and

- occupied for no more than 31 days by the same person in any period of seven months.

 ## 62 Assets you can sell without incurring Capital Gains Tax

You can sell chattels such as jewellery, pictures and furniture where the proceeds are £6,000 or less without incurring Capital Gains Tax. Please note that if you sell, say, a set of chairs for more than £6,000, you cannot claim this as being free from Capital Gains Tax on the basis that each individual chair was sold for less than £6,000. HMRC looks at the set as an item, not the individual items themselves. There are other assets you can sell (or gains you can make) without incurring Capital Gains Tax:

- Private motor vehicles
- Your own home (but not including a second home)
- National Savings Certificates
- Foreign currency
- Some gold coins (take advice)
- Decorations for gallantry (unless purchased)
- Betting winnings (including pools, lotteries and premium bonds)
- Compensation or damages for any wrong or injury suffered
- British Government Securities
- Life assurance policies and deferred annuities
- Chattels (i.e. movable possessions) sold for £6,000 or less
- Assets given to a charity or the nation
- Enterprise Investment Scheme shares held for three years
- Investments held in Individual Savings Accounts
- Guns, wine, antiques – providing they are not used in a business
- Debts
- Qualifying Corporate Bonds
- Child Trust Funds

##  Enterprise Investment Scheme (EISs)

In addition to the Income Tax relief (see number 9), there are two valuable Capital Gains Tax exemptions. Firstly, provided that the EIS shares have been held for at least three years, when the shares are sold at a profit there is no charge to Capital Gains Tax.

Secondly, if you have a Capital Gains Tax liability, an investment into EIS shares can be used to defer that gain. A claim may be made for any or all of a chargeable gain arising from any source (subject to the annual investment limits) to be invested into EIS shares within one year before, and three years after the disposal. The effect of this is that the capital gain is deferred. The deferred gain doesn't become chargeable until the EIS shares are sold or until the EIS investment ceases to be eligible (see conditions above). However, where the hitherto deferred gain becomes chargeable, it can be further deferred by the making of a further EIS investment.

Deferred gains don't become chargeable on the death of the investor.

##  64 Seed Enterprise Investment Scheme (SEIS)

Like EIS investments, SEIS investments will be free from Capital Gains Tax when sold, provided that they have been held for at least three years. In addition, any taxpayer who has a Capital Gains Tax liability will receive 50 per cent CGT relief when they reinvest those gains into seed companies.

##  65 Venture Capital Trusts (VCTs)

Gains arising on the disposal of VCT shares are exempt from CGT and there is no minimum period for which they must be held.

##  66 Other investments with tax advantages

While it's not our business to suggest individual investments, the following investments have certain tax advantages:

- **National Savings Certificates:** These are lump sum investments that earn guaranteed rates of interest over set terms

- **Children's Bonds:** These are high-interest savings schemes for children under the age of 16. You can get a brochure at any post office and both the interest and the bonus are tax free.

- **Individual Savings Accounts (ISAs):** These are financial products designed for the purpose of investment and savings. Money is contributed from after-tax income and not subjected to Income Tax or Capital Gains Tax within a holding or upon withdrawal. Cash and a broad range of investments can be held, and there is no restriction on when or how much money can be withdrawn. Funds cannot be used as security for a loan. It is not a pension product but can be a useful complement to a pension for retirement income.

---

 ## It can be a good idea to crystallise capital gains if there is going to be no tax to pay

Each year, you are entitled to make tax-free capital gains of £11,100. If you have not made any gains and have (say) some shares that, if you were to sell, would achieve a taxable gain of no more than £11,100, it would make sense to sell them and then buy them back (if you wanted to keep the shares) because you would then have them at a higher cost of acquisition and if you were to sell them again in the future, this would reduce or possibly eliminate any taxable gain when that happens. If you do buy the shares back, you have to wait for 30 days to do so, otherwise anti-avoidance rules come into play.

---

 ## Claim Rollover Relief

If you make a gain on the sale of a qualifying business asset, and reinvest the proceeds in a new qualifying business asset, within the period starting one year before and ending three years after the original disposal, a claim may be made to have the gain deferred.

Qualifying business assets include land and buildings (including property which qualifies as furnished holiday lettings); plant and machinery; ships; aircraft; hovercraft; goodwill; milk, potato and fish quotas; ewe and suckler cow premium quotas; payment entitlements under the farmers' single payment scheme and Lloyd's syndicate rights.

For the very adventurous business person, satellites, space stations and spacecraft are also included!

The replacement asset doesn't have to be within the same category as the asset sold.

Where only some of the sale proceeds are reinvested, the remaining part of the gain is immediately chargeable.

 ## Time your sales to defer payment of Capital Gains Tax

A tax deferred gives you a cash-flow advantage, so it makes sense to delay the due date for paying tax whenever you can. If you sell an asset on 5 April, you will have to pay the Capital Gains Tax ten months later. If you delay the sale by just one day and sell on 6 April, the Capital Gains Tax doesn't have to be paid for 22 months. Don't forget the date of sale for Capital Gains Tax purposes is the date you exchange contracts and not the completion date.

 ## Reduce or eliminate Capital Gains Tax on a second home

If you are about to purchase or have purchased a second home, you can elect (within two years from buying the second one) which is to be the principal private residence for Capital Gains Tax purposes. This is a complex area and it's recommended that you take professional advice.

A further consideration worth looking into would be if you are selling a second home and there is tax to pay, could you occupy it for a short time as your main residence as this may reduce the tax payable? You would get a minimum of 18 months' worth of Private Residence Relief (but you would genuinely need to move in for a period).

There is also a valuable allowance available where your main residence has been let. This exemption for letting as residential accommodation is worth £40,000 or the amount of the gain attributable to the period of residence if that is less. This allowance is available to both a husband and wife or both partners in a civil partnership if they are joint owners.

# CHAPTER 11
# Inheritance Tax

## 71 Check-up to see what your Inheritance Tax is likely to be

| I own | Estimated value | At my death I would like to leave this to: |
|---|---|---|
| House | | |
| Valuables | | |
| Shares* | | |
| Cash | | |
| Other land and property | | |
| Trust | | |
| Business assets* | | |
| The residue of my estate | | |
| Legacies I would like to give | | Details: |
| Substantial gifts I have made in the last seven years | | Gifted to: |
| *Less* Sums I owe | ( ) | How will these be repaid on death? |
| **Total estate** | | |
| **Less tax-free band** | **(£325,000)** | |
| **Less unused tax-free band of deceased spouse/civil partner** | **(x)** | |
| **Total net** | | |
| **Tax due @ 40%** | | |

\* Some shares (those listed on the Alternative Investment Market and shares in unlisted companies) and business assets will attract 100 per cent business property relief and be effectively free of Inheritance Tax.

**72** ## What gifts are exempt from Inheritance Tax?

Many gifts are exempt from tax so make use of these exemptions.

• Gifts between spouses and civil partners, but if one is not UK domiciled, the lifetime exemption is limited to £325,000.

• Gifts of up to £3,000 in each tax year are exempt and the unused portion of the previous year's exemption can be carried forward but only for one year.

• A gift of £250 to any one person if the total gifts to that person don't exceed £250. This can be used to cover Christmas and birthday gifts from grandparents to grandchildren.

• Wedding gifts of up to:

    • £5,000 from each parent to each child;

    • £2,500 from each grandparent;

    • £1,000 from anybody else.

    The gift must be made shortly before the marriage and becomes effective when the marriage takes place.

• If you have surplus income year on year, this can be gifted free of Inheritance Tax. You need to be able to show that such gifts are part of your regular annual expenditure and don't reduce your standard of living. The exemption can be used if you pay life insurance premiums for the benefit of someone else. You should keep a record of these gifts and if possible a record of your net (after tax) income. This can be a very useful exemption as there is no upper limit so it's worth keeping the documentation.

• Gifts to UK charities, political parties (providing they have at least one MP and 150,000 votes), registered housing associations and gifts for national purposes are also exempt.

• Maintenance payments to your dependants and ex-spouse.

If the gift is not covered by any of these exemptions, then providing you survive for seven years it will be free of Inheritance Tax.

For deaths on or after 6 April 2012, estates including charitable legacies of at least ten per cent of the net estate will benefit from a 36 per cent rate of IHT.

Since 19 March 2014, the estates of armed forces personnel have been exempt from IHT, where their deaths have been caused or hastened by injury while on active service. This exemption has now been extended to emergency services personnel and humanitarian aid workers responding to emergency circumstances.

##  Inheritance Tax business/agricultural property relief

Certain categories of business and business assets may qualify for 100 per cent exemption from Inheritance Tax after two years. The relief normally applies to a business or an interest in a business (partnership) or to shares in an unlisted company. Shares quoted on the Alternative Investment Market (AIM) also qualify after two years. The exemption also applies to farmers after two years if they farm the land and after seven years if the farm is let to someone else who farms the land. Full details of these reliefs are beyond the scope of this book and professional advice should be taken.

##  Changes to the tax-free band

Married couples or registered civil partners can use each other's unused element of the nil-rate band on first death. So, for 2015/16 a couple have a joint nil-rate band of £650,000. If the couple's joint estate falls within the joint nil-rate band, they do not have to worry about Inheritance Tax.

For everyone else, including unmarried couples, siblings living together and carers who have lived with and inherited the family home, the nil-rate band is £325,000 for 2015/16.

# CHAPTER 12
# Overseas aspects

**75.** Can you save tax by going abroad?

##  75 Can you save tax by going abroad?

### Residence, domicile, etc.

The overseas aspect of UK taxation is a complex area, but, in general terms, if you are a UK resident, you will be liable to pay UK tax on your worldwide income. If you are not a UK resident, you will only be liable to pay UK tax on income arising in the UK.

Without wanting to make matters too complex, reference will be made to the terms *residence, ordinary residence* and *domicile.*

### What is the Statutory Residence Test?

The Statutory Residence Test has been designed to provide greater certainty as to whether or not individuals are UK resident for tax purposes. This test does not have retrospective effect, but it could be the case that somebody who has previously been non-UK-resident becomes UK-resident following the introduction of this test.

There are a number of stages to the test and a variety of rules to apply to determine an individual's status. It is split into a number of components:

- Automatic Overseas Tests
- Automatic Residence Tests
- Sufficient Ties Test

The basic rules are that you are non-UK-resident in a tax year if you meet any of the Automatic Overseas Tests. But you are UK-resident if you do not meet any of the Automatic Overseas Tests and you meet one of the Automatic Residence Tests, or the Sufficient TiesTest.

## Automatic Overseas Tests

If you meet any one of these tests, you are non-UK-resident:

**1.** You were resident in the UK for one or more of the previous three tax years and you spend fewer than 16 days in the UK in the tax year.

**2.** You were not resident in the UK for any of the three preceding tax years and you spend fewer than 46 days in the UK in the tax year.

**3.** You work full-time overseas throughout the tax year without any significant breaks, and:

**a.** you spend fewer than 91 days in the UK in the tax year;

**b.** the number of days in the tax year on which you work for more than three hours in the UK is less than 31.

If, having taken this test, you are not conclusively non-resident, then you must move on to the Automatic Residence Test.

## Automatic Residence Test

If you meet any one of these tests, you will be automatically UK-resident:

**1.** You spend 183 days of more in the UK in the tax year.

**2.** You have a home in the UK during all or part of the tax year. You will meet this test if there is at least one period of 91 consecutive days, at least 30 of which fall into the tax year, when you have a home in the UK in which you spend a sufficient amount of time and either you:

**a.** have no overseas home, or

**b.** have an overseas home or homes in each of which you spend no more than a permitted amount of time.

If you have more than one home in the UK, you should consider each of those homes separately to see if you meet the test. You need only meet this test in relation to one of your UK homes.

**3.** You work full-time in the UK for any period of 365 days, with no significant break from UK work, and:

**a.** all, or part, of that 365-day period falls within the tax year;

**b.** more than 75 per cent of the total number of days in the 365-day period when you do more than three hours of work are days when you do more than three hours work in the UK;

**c.** at least one day which is both in the 365-day period and in the tax year is a day on which you do more than three hours of work in the UK.

## Sufficient Ties Test

If you do not meet any of the Automatic Overseas Tests or any of the Automatic Residence Tests, you should use the Sufficient Ties Test to determine your UK residence status for a tax year. You will need to consider your connections to the UK, called ties, and determine whether your ties, taken together with the number of days you spend in the UK, are sufficient for you to be considered UK-resident for tax purposes for a particular tax year.

If you were not UK-resident for any of the three tax years before the tax year under consideration, you will need to consider if you have any of these UK ties:

1. Family: spouse, civil partner, partner, or minor children, in the UK

2. Accommodation: having accommodation in the UK which is available for a continuous period of at least 91 days and you spend at least one night there.

3. Substantive work in the UK: 40 working days or more (a working day is defined as more than three hours of work).

4. UK presence in the previous two tax years: more than 90 days in either of the previous two tax years.

5. More days spent in the UK in a tax year than in any other single country: this applies to leavers only and is designed to catch leavers who do not take up residence in any other country following a period of UK residence.

The number of days you spend in the UK in a tax year will dictate the number of UK ties that are needed for you to be UK resident.

| Days in UK | Arrivers – not resident in the UK in previous three tax years | Leavers – resident in the UK in at least one of the previous three tax years |
|---|---|---|
| Less than 16 | Always non resident | Always non resident |
| 16 – 45 days | Always non resident | Resident only if at least four ties apply |
| 46 – 90 days | Resident only if at least four ties apply | Resident only if at least three ties apply |

| 91 – 120 days | Resident only if at least three ties apply | Resident only if at least two ties apply |
| --- | --- | --- |
| 121 – 182 days | Resident only if at least two ties apply | Resident only if at least one tie applies |
| 183 days or more | Always resident | Always resident |

# Domicile

A person's domicile is usually the country in which they have their permanent home and other related connections. When you are born you usually take your father's domicile (*domicile of origin*). Until you are able to change it, you will follow the domicile of the person on whom you are dependent (*domicile of dependency*). It's also possible to change your domicile by moving to another country and thoroughly embedding yourself within the society and culture (*domicile of choice*). There are high standards of proof for this, however.

The domicile of married women is determined independently of their husband.

# Split-year treatment

Under the Statutory Residence Test. you are either UK resident or non UK resident for a full tax year and at all times in that tax year. However, if during a year you either start to live or work abroad or come from abroad to live or work in the UK, the tax year will be split into two parts if your circumstances meet specific criteria:

• A UK part for which you are charged to UK tax as a UK resident.

• An overseas part which, for most purposes, you are charged to UK tax as a non UK resident.

This is a complex area, so if this scenario might apply to your own circumstances, it is important to seek advice from a professional.

# Remittance basis charge

If you are resident but not domiciled in the UK, and a Commonwealth citizen (includes UK), or a citizen of the Republic of Ireland, you will be taxed on income remitted to the UK (i.e. paid to the UK). Because this was seen as a way of avoiding tax, those wishing to pay tax on the remittance basis who have been resident in the UK for more than seven of the past nine years, now have to pay an annual charge of £30,000. From 6 April 2015, there is an increase in this annual charge to £60,000 for non-domiciled individuals who have been UK-resident for 12 of the past 14 years. There will also be a new charge of £90,000 for those who have been resident for 17 out of the last 20 years.

## Other aspects

- Non-residents cannot claim UK personal allowances unless they are UK, Commonwealth or Republic of Ireland citizens or EEA nationals (EU countries plus Iceland, Norway and Liechtenstein).

- If you are UK resident and domiciled and in receipt of a pension from overseas, you can claim a ten per cent deduction on the amount of pension liable to tax in the UK.

- People becoming non-resident in the UK (also those whose place of abode moves overseas) but retaining a property here which is going to be let out become non-resident landlords. HMRC needs to be notified on Form NRL1. HMRC can authorise the rents to be paid without the deduction of basic-rate tax, by the letting agent or the tenant, which is what should happen automatically. Provided the landlord is within one of the categories above, a claim for UK personal allowances can be made to minimise tax liabilities.

- Non-residents who are in receipt of the UK state pension can disclaim personal allowances and have the full amount of state pension removed from their tax liability calculations.

- If an individual left the UK after 17 March 1998 and has been non-resident for five complete tax years from the date of departure, there is no liability to Capital Gains Tax on assets sold prior to their return to the UK. From 6 April 2015, this exemption no longer applies to residential property; the non-resident will become liable to gains on residential property which have arisen from 6 April 2015, not those arising over the whole period of ownership of the property. It may be worthwhile getting professional valuations prepared of all such UK residential property, so that when they come to be sold, an accurate capital gains computation can be prepared.

## Scope of liability to Income Tax of earnings

| | Residence status and domicile | Duties of employment performed wholly or partly in the UK | | Duties of employment performed wholly outside the UK |
|---|---|---|---|---|
| | | *In the UK* | *Outside the UK* | |
| **Foreign emoluments**[1] | Employee resident and ordinarily resident in the UK | Liable – less possible deduction[2] | Liable – less possible deduction[2] | Liable if received in the UK[3] |
| | Resident but not ordinarily resident | Liable | Liable if received in the UK[3] | Liable if received in the UK[3] |
| | Not resident | Liable | Not liable | Not liable |
| **Other earnings** | Resident and ordinarily resident | Liable – less possible deduction[2] | Liable – less possible deduction[2] | Liable – less possible deduction[2] |
| | Resident but not ordinarily resident | Liable | Liable if received in the UK[3] | Liable if received in the UK[3] |
| | Not resident | Liable | Not liable | Not liable |

1. 'Foreign emoluments' is the term used in the Taxes Act to mean the earnings of someone who is not domiciled in the UK and whose employer is resident outside, and not resident in, the UK (nor resident in the Republic of Ireland).

2. There may be a foreign earnings deduction of 100 per cent in these cases from the amount chargeable, if the earnings are for a period which is part of a qualifying absence lasting 365 days or more – this means that such earnings for that period will be free from UK tax. This only applies to seafarers.

3. The remittance basis which applies in these cases. See above.

## Scope of liability to Income Tax on individuals receiving pensions

| Residence status and domicile | Paid by or on behalf of a person | |
| --- | --- | --- |
| | *In the UK* | *Outside the UK (Overseas Pension)* |
| Resident and ordinarily resident, and domiciled | Liable | Liable[1] |
| Resident and ordinarily resident, not domiciled | Liable | Liable if received in the UK[2,3] |
| Resident but not ordinarily resident, domiciled | Liable | Liable[1,4] |
| Resident but not ordinarily resident, not domiciled | Liable | Liable if received in the UK[2,3] |
| Not resident | Liable [5,6] | Not liable |

1. Less ten per cent deduction.

2. You are taxable on the whole of a pension arising in the Republic of Ireland, less ten per cent deduction, but if the pension is from the Irish Government, you are taxable only if you are a UK national without also being an Irish national.

3. If you are not UK domiciled and opt for the remittance basis of taxation, there may be an annual charge. See page 82.

4. If you are a Commonwealth (this includes British) citizen or an Irish citizen, the remittance basis applies and the ten per cent deduction is not due, unless the pension arises in the Irish Republic, in which case note 2 applies.

5. There may be relief under a double taxation agreement.

6. It may be beneficial not to claim UK personal allowances.

## Scope of liability to Income Tax on profits of individuals carrying on a trade or profession

| | Trade or profession carried on wholly or partly in the UK | Trade or profession carried on wholly outside the UK |
|---|---|---|
| **Residence status and domicile** | | |
| Resident and ordinarily resident, and domiciled | Liable | Liable |
| Resident and ordinarily resident, not domiciled | Liable | Liable if received in the UK[1, 4] |
| Resident but not ordinarily resident, domiciled | Liable | Liable[2] |
| Resident but not ordinarily resident, not domiciled | Liable | Liable if received in the UK[1, 4] |
| Not resident | Liable[3] | Not liable |

1.  You are taxable on the whole of the income from a trade or profession carried on wholly in the Republic of Ireland.

2.  If you are a Commonwealth (this includes British) citizen or an Irish citizen, the remittance basis applies unless the trade or profession is carried on wholly in the Irish Republic, in which case note 1 applies.

3.  You are liable on the profits of the part of the trade or profession carried on in the UK.

4.  If you are not UK domiciled and opt for the remittance basis of taxation, there may be an annual charge. See page 82.

# CHAPTER 13
# When someone dies

## Don't overpay Inheritance Tax on assets that are sold

Inheritance Tax is a damaging tax. Not only is the rate high (40 per cent) and the sums payable tend to have a great many noughts after them, but, on top of this, the tax has to be paid from a bank account that probably has no cash in it with which to pay the tax.

There are few ameliorations of this dreadful state of affairs but there is one and it's often overlooked.

Inheritance Tax is paid on the probate value of the assets. This is the professional value that is put on the assets as at the date of death. But if you sell certain of these assets within either four years of death for land and property (one year for quoted securities) and they realise a sum that is lower than probate value, you can apply to the Capital Taxes Office for a refund of 40 per cent of the difference between the two. You can only get the relief if there is an overall loss on the sale of quoted securities. The relief is not due solely on the shares that have realised a loss.

If the asset is sold for a sum higher than probate value, then Capital Gains Tax may be payable.

 ## Remember to claim full probate costs when someone dies

When an asset is to be sold by the personal representatives of the deceased, the cost for the purpose of Capital Gains Tax will be its probate value. This can be increased further to make some allowance for probate costs. The amount allowed is based on the size of the estate and ranges from 1.8 per cent if the estate is valued at up to £50,000 to 0.16 per cent for estates valued over £5,000,000, subject to a maximum of £10,000.

## Capital Gains Tax and Inheritance Tax considerations

If elderly people are considering giving away their assets to reduce Inheritance Tax, bear in mind that there is no Capital Gains Tax to pay on death and the beneficiaries will inherit assets at probate value. This could be considerably higher than the value at the time of the gift so the beneficiaries may be able to sell the asset after death without incurring Capital Gains Tax. This needs careful planning as you could end up paying more Inheritance Tax than the Capital Gains Tax saved.

If an asset that belonged to someone who has died is sold, there could be Capital Gains Tax due on the gain, but personal representatives of deceased persons can claim the annual exemption (£11,100 for 2015/16) for not only the tax year of death but also the following two years. Thereafter, no exemption is available.

 ## Should I consider a deed of variation?

If all the beneficiaries of a deceased estate are in agreement, it is possible for a deed of variation to be drawn up. This effectively changes the wishes expressed in the Will. Changes can be made which are more tax efficient; for instance, leaving money to a charity. Legal advice should be sought on the matter.

# CHAPTER 14
# Pensions

**80.** Take out a pension

**81.** You may be able to take out a pension even if you are not earning

**82.** Maximise your tax-free lump sum entitlement

**83.** Always take independent advice before drawing your pension

## (80) Take out a pension

If you contribute to a pension scheme, the government will add a further £2.50 for every £10 you pay. For higher-rate taxpayers, the government contribution increases to £6.66, and for additional-rate taxpayers, to £9. Once invested, the money grows in a tax-free environment. In 2015/16, the annual maximum that can be paid into a personal pension is £40,000.

If you have not fully used your annual maximum in the previous three years, providing the scheme was in existence the unused relief can be carried forward, permitting payments in a given year exceeding the annual £40,000 limit.

## (81) Taking out a pension even if you're not earning

Stakeholder pensions are not just for workers; non-earning spouses and children can have them and benefit from 20 per cent tax relief. So for higher-rate taxpayers, this is a useful way of sheltering your capital from Income Tax and investing it in a tax-free environment for the benefit of your family. The maximum contribution is £3,600 per annum before tax relief, equating to a net payment of £2,880.

## (82) Maximise your tax-free lump sum entitlement

When you come to draw your personal pension, you will be entitled to take a tax-free lump sum of 25 per cent of the value of your pension fund. This option should be given careful consideration, because it is tax free, whereas the annuity income that you are using your fund to purchase will be taxable, as will draw down income if you choose that option.

## (83) Always take independent financial advice

When your personal pension reaches maturity, you have various options. Different companies offer different products and rates, so it is important to get independent financial advice on this. If you have any health conditions, this could enable you to get an even better return on your investment.

The significant changes in the 2014 and 2015 Budgets relating to the full availability of your pension pot and converting existing annuities into cash make it more important than ever that sound advice be taken on the options available. The government has introduced a generic online advice service at www.pensionswise.gov.uk. However, we urge that independent financial advice, tailored to your circumstances, be taken on this complex subject; although not free, it could pay for itself many times over.

# CHAPTER 15
# Property

##  84  Rent a room

You can receive gross rents of up to £4,250 tax free per year for letting furnished rooms in your own home. If you own two properties, the relief only applies to the main family home. If the property is jointly owned, the relief is divided between you. Should the rent you receive exceed this amount, you have two choices. You can choose to pay tax on the excess rent over £4,250 or on the rent you receive less the expenses. You have to make a claim if you want to pay on the excess over £4,250 and this basis will apply until you withdraw the claim. This relief is usually used when people take in lodgers so it won't apply if the rooms you let constitute a flat with its own facilities. If the rent is within the rent-a-room scheme, there won't be any Capital Gains Tax issues if you ever sell your house. The relief is also available to people running a bed & breakfast business.

The relief is not just for owner-occupiers. If you are a tenant in rented accommodation, you will also qualify if you sublet a room, providing that it's your main home.

It's advisable to tell your mortgage company and your insurers if you enter into a rent-a-room arrangement.

## 85  VAT and rent

If you are VAT registered and you also have rental income, you are making what the VAT man calls an 'exempt' supply. You cannot charge VAT on the rent and equally you cannot reclaim VAT on the property expenses. Normally, a partly exempt business has to use a special method to work out how much input VAT it can reclaim. However, if the input tax on the property expenses in any VAT period is not more than:

1. £625 per month on average; and
2. one half of all input tax for the period concerned;

all the input tax on the property expenses can be reclaimed.

The above doesn't apply if you receive rents from non-domestic property and you have opted to tax the property.

## 86 Have you claimed for all the expenses you can?

See the template on the following page for guidance on expenditure types.

## 87 Claim the interest on any loan you take out to buy the property

If you borrow money to buy a property to let, you will get tax relief on the interest you pay at your top rate of tax. You can also get tax relief on loans to fund improvements, alterations or repairs.

There is an interesting addition to the manuals of HM Revenue & Customs (HMRC) which indicates that interest on funds borrowed for private purposes may be deductible against rental income in certain circumstances. This has wide-reaching implications for buy-to-let investors.

One example in the manual covers Mr A, who owns a flat in London and is moving abroad. He decides to let the property while he is away. During his period of ownership, the property has trebled in value. He renegotiates the mortgage to convert it to a buy-to-let mortgage and borrows a further amount which he uses to buy a property overseas. Can he claim tax relief on the interest against the rents? Well, HMRC says that owners of businesses (and renting property is a business for tax purposes) are entitled to withdraw their capital from the business, even though substitute funding then has to be provided by interest-bearing loans. In the case of Mr A, his opening balance sheet shows the following:

| | | | |
|---|---|---|---|
| **Original mortgage** | 80,000 | **Property at market value** | 375,000 |
| **Capital account** | 295,000 | | |
| | £375,000 | | £375,000 |

When Mr A renegotiates his mortgage, he borrows a further £125,000, which goes through his property business. He then withdraws this amount to fund the purchase of the property overseas. By the end of the first year of letting, his balance sheet shows the following.

## A template to help you prepare your figures for the Land and Property pages of the Tax Return

Your name _____

## Land and property income (year to 5 April    )

**Income**   Received from                                            Rents received
£

_____

_____

_____

                                          Total income   £

                     Tax already deducted from property income   £

                                                    £          £

**Expenditure**                      **Premises**  Rents   _____
                                          Rates   _____
                              Property insurance   _____
                                   Light and heat   _____
                                        Cleaning   _____
                                        Security   _____
                                                   Subtotal   [        ]

                  **Repairs and maintenance**  Repairs and renewals   _____
                                     Redecorating   _____
                                      Small tools   _____
                                                   Subtotal   [        ]

**Finance charges and interest** on loan to buy rented property   [        ]

                       **Legal and professional**  Legal   _____
                                     Accountancy   _____
                                  Debt collection   _____
                                  Other insurances   _____
                                    Subscriptions   _____
                                    Architects' fees   _____
                                                   Subtotal   [        ]

                           **Services provided**  Wages   _____
                                       Telephone   _____
                                             TV   _____
                                          Garden   _____
                                          Roads   _____
                                                   Subtotal   [        ]

                            **Other costs**  Advertising   _____
                                      Agents' fees   _____
                                      Office costs   _____
                                          Travel   _____
                                                   Subtotal   [        ]

                                          Total expenditure   [ £        ]

| | | | |
|---|---|---|---|
| **Mortgage** | 205,000 | **Property at market value** | 375,000 |
| **Capital account b/f** | 295,000 | | |
| **Less drawings** | (125,000) | | |
| **Carry forward** | 170,000 | | |
| | £375,000 | | £375,000 |

Although he has withdrawn capital from the business, the interest on the mortgage loan is allowable in full because it's funding the transfer of the property to the business at its open market value at the time the business started. Although HMRC's example has a further mortgage of £125,000, it seems that Mr A could withdraw a further £170,000 of tax-allowable finance. However, he should not take out more than he puts in as his capital account will be in the red (i.e. overdrawn).

The best advice is not to assume that you will automatically get tax relief but to take professional advice before you remortgage.

## 88 Do you and your spouse/civil partner jointly own the property?

If a married couple or civil partners own a property in joint names (joint tenancy), the income and expenditure is always divided equally when filling in the Tax Return forms. However, if the ownership is owned as tenants in common and if you ask the tax office for Form 17 ('Declaration of beneficial interests in joint property and income'), you can jointly declare the ownership split that actually applies and then you can enter those amounts on the Tax Returns; for instance, it may be that the property is owned 60:40 and this would be the mechanism to get the income from it split on the same basis.

## 89 Forestry

Forestry can be a good way to save tax. In principle, there are three main advantages:

1. There is no Inheritance Tax on forestry property.

2. There is no Income Tax on forestry income.

3. When it comes to forestry sales, only the gain on the sale of the land, not the growing timber, attracts Capital Gains Tax.

There may not be much money in forestry, but at least there's virtually no tax either!

# CHAPTER 16
# Savings and investments

## 90 Get your interest paid gross

If you are not a taxpayer, i.e. your annual taxable income is less than your personal allowances, you can elect to have any bank or building society interest you receive paid without tax being deducted. In the majority of cases, and in the absence of such an election, interest is paid after 20 per cent tax has been deducted and it's 'net' interest rather than 'gross'. If you are not a taxpayer (or only have investment income within the £5,000, 0% tax band) but have been taxed on your interest, you will be due a refund. There are plans for this automatic deduction of interest to be abolished from 6 April 2016 which, in conjunction with other changes announced, will simplify matters for the majority of taxpayers.

 ## 91 Individual Savings Accounts (ISAs)

ISAs allow interest to be paid tax free. Shares can also be held in an ISA; dividends on these are tax free and they can be sold free of Capital Gains Tax. From 6 April 2015, the annual ISA investment limit is £15,240. There is no longer any limit to the amount which can be held in cash. The limit for a Junior ISA is £4,080 In the Autumn of 2015, details will be announced of how the rules covering money put in and taken out are going to be relaxed. Also, from 3 December 2014, if an ISA holder dies they will be able to pass on the ISA benefits to their surviving spouse or civil partner.

## Help to Buy ISA

From the Autumn of 2015, a new type of ISA account will be available aimed at first-time property buyers. Further details will be announced in due course, but in general terms it will be possible to save up to £200 per month and if you saved £12,000 you would receive a bonus of £3,000 from the government. This only applies provided that the money is used to buy a home in the UK costing under £450,000 in London, or £250,000 elsewhere.

##  92 National Savings and Investments (NSI)

A range of National Savings investments is available, but these can mean locking your capital away for a fixed period and there is also a maximum amount that can be invested each year. National Savings Certificates should be considered, as the interest is tax free and, therefore, particularly attractive to higher-rate taxpayers. Pensioners born before 6 April 1948 who would have their age-related allowances reduced by receiving taxable income should also consider tax-free investments (those with taxable incomes over £27,700 in 2015/16).

A range of fixed-rate bonds for those aged 65 and over were introduced in January 2015, with a maximum holding of £10,000 per person. The interest rates to be paid are 2.8 per cent for the one-year bond and 4 per cent for the three-year bond.

##  93 Premium Bonds

If you like a flutter but don't want to risk your capital, Premium Bonds may be for you. The minimum investment is £100 and the maximum holding was £40,000; from 1 June 2015, this maximum increased to £50,000. The monthly draw results in prizes of various amounts which are tax free. As well as a £1 million jackpot, you can win anything from £25 to £100,000 for each bond number you hold. You can encash the bonds at any time for their face value.

# CHAPTER 17
# Charitable giving

## 94 Gift Aid

If you 'Gift Aid' a donation to charity, the charity claims back the basic-rate tax that is deemed to have been deducted from the grossed-up payment. Therefore, for every pound you Gift Aid to charity, the charity claims an additional 25p. You must have paid at least 25p in tax yourself. If you have not done so, then you will owe HMRC the amount the charity has claimed.

In addition to feeling good about your generosity, if you are a higher-rate or additional-rate taxpayer, you are also entitled to tax relief at an additional 20 or 25 per cent on your donation. This is achieved by extending your basic-rate band, i.e. more of your income is charged to tax at 20 per cent rather than 40 or 45 per cent. You can also elect for your gift to be treated as paid in the previous tax year so that higher-rate or additional-rate relief can be claimed in that year.

Gift Aid payments can be used very effectively to avoid having income falling in the range £100,000 to £121,200, where the marginal rate can be as high as 62%, and £50,000 to £60,000, where entitlement to child benefit is lost.

## 95 Charities

As well as cash gifts to charities, tax relief is also available on gifts of shares, securities (including AIM shares, unit trusts, etc.) and land and buildings. Individuals will get Income Tax relief on the market value of the gift on the date of the gift, plus any incidental costs of disposal or transfer, less any consideration or benefit received, at their top rate of tax. In addition, companies can claim relief. Such gifts to charities are exempt from Capital Gains Tax so neither a chargeable gain nor allowable loss will arise. Care is needed if the gift is a building on which capital allowances have been claimed as this is likely to result in a tax liability which would reduce the value of the tax relief otherwise due.

# CHAPTER 18
# Marriage and children

## Give children assets when they are not worth very much

This is one of those points which, while obvious, often gets overlooked. Let's say that you are setting up a new business and it's to be a limited company. (This is not the only sort of opportunity to which this idea might relate but it happens to make the point very well.) So you have just incorporated the business, it hasn't yet traded and it is worth extremely little. If you were to issue some shares to your children on day one and if we assume that the business does well and in a few years' time it's worth a tidy sum of money, the capital growth on the children's shares will all belong to them.

If, however, you delay giving them the shares, then when you transfer them to the children, you may have to pay Capital Gains Tax on any gain you make on the disposal.

## 97 What are the best investments for children?

The simplest answer is that savings accounts with building societies or banks that are in the children's names should pay the children interest gross (i.e. without tax deducted).

If the children don't have any investments and if the parents have surplus after-tax income of their own which they give to their children, this is usually tax free in the children's hands and, if the parents are particularly wealthy, is a very useful way of transferring income to them, so that the children can accumulate a sum that can then be invested. However, once the income from the source exceeds £100 per annum, it will be taxed in the hands of the parents. If parents transfer their own shares to their children and the children are under 18, the income arising on these shares will be regarded as belonging to the parents, so this doesn't save tax.

Junior ISAs are a long-term tax-free savings vehicle for children. Your child can have a Junior ISA if they are under 18, live in the UK and do not already have a Child Trust Fund account. Each child can have one cash and one stocks and shares Junior ISA at any one time. The limit is £4,080 from 6 April 2015.

## 98 Plan separation and divorce carefully

Assets transferred between married couples and civil partners who are living together are exempt from Capital Gains Tax. This exemption also applies in the tax year in which they separate. Arranging for the division and transfer of assets can be a time-consuming process and it's not always possible to finalise this before the end of the tax year of separation, even if separation occurs very early in the tax year. When assets are transferred after the year of separation, Capital Gains Tax is charged in the normal way. This should be borne in mind when considering a matrimonial settlement.

# CHAPTER 19
# And finally ...

## 99 Free HMRC explanatory publications – a good source of tax information

Most, if not all, leaflets can be accessed via the HM Revenue & Customs (HMRC) website (www.gov.uk/government/organisations/hm-revenue-customs).

It's strongly recommended that your starting point should be a phone call to the number shown on any correspondence you have received from HMRC, or from your telephone directory. This may be a frustrating experience, as there have been reports of long waiting times for calls to be answered. However, a word of warning: if you are expecting HMRC staff to offer a free accountancy/taxation service, you will be very disappointed.

The HMRC website lists the following types of publication:

### Tax information and impact notes

These communicate all tax policy changes and include an explanation of what we are doing, why, and what impact it has for both customers and HMRC

### Notices, information sheets and other reference materials

Public Notices, Notes, Information Sheets, Fact Sheets and related documents across all tax areas

### Revenue & Customs Briefs

Revenue & Customs Briefs issued by HM Revenue & Customs in date order or by subject matter

### Leaflets and booklets

All current leaflets & booklets published by HM Revenue & Customs

### Budget and pre-Budget reports

Budget and pre-Budget publications and news releases issued by HM Revenue & Customs

## Specialist publications

Recently published technical guides, reports and specialist information

## Extra-statutory concessions and statements of practice

How HM Revenue & Customs interprets the law and applies it in practice especially where a strict interpretation would have unintended consequences

## Banking Code of Practice

HMRC publishes its Governance Protocol on the Code of Practice on Taxation for Banks, along with updated figures on adoption of the Code

# Helpsheets

HMRC publishes a number of helpful guides and leaflets. SA150 is called 'How to fill in your Tax Return' and is updated for each tax year. HMRC also publishes a number of helpsheets. These are available from the SA orderline on 0300 200 3610 or you can download them from www.gov.uk/government/collections/hmrc-forms.

### For page TR 3 of the Tax Return

| | |
|---|---|
| Helpsheet 310 | War widow's and dependant's pensions |

### For page TR 4 of the Tax Return

| | |
|---|---|
| Helpsheet 347 | Personal term assurance contributions to a registered pension scheme |

### For the *Additional information* pages

| | |
|---|---|
| Helpsheet 237 | Community Investment Tax Relief |
| Helpsheet 305 | Employee shares and securities – further guidance |
| Helpsheet 320 | Gains on UK life insurance policies |
| Helpsheet 325 | Other taxable income |
| Helpsheet 340 | Interest and alternative finance payments eligible for relief on qualifying loans and alternative finance arrangements |
| Helpsheet 341 | Enterprise Investment Scheme – Income Tax relief |
| Helpsheet 342 | Charitable giving |
| Helpsheet 343 | Accrued Income Scheme |

| Helpsheet 344 | Exempt employers' contributions to an overseas pension scheme |
|---|---|
| Helpsheet 345 | Pensions – tax charges on any excess over the Lifetime Allowance, Annual Allowance and Special Annual Allowance, and on unauthorised payments |
| Helpsheet 346 | Pension savings tax charges – guidance for members of overseas pension schemes that are not UK registered pension schemes |

### For the *Employment* pages

| Helpsheet 201 | Vouchers, credit cards and tokens |
|---|---|
| Helpsheet 202 | Living accommodation |
| Helpsheet 203 | Car benefits and car fuel benefits |
| Helpsheet 205 | Seafarers' Earnings Deduction |
| Helpsheet 207 | Non-taxable payments or benefits for employees |
| Helpsheet 208 | Payslips and coding notices |
| Helpsheet 210 | Assets provided for private use |
| Helpsheet 211 | Employment – residence and domicile issues |
| Helpsheet 212 | Tax equalisation |
| Helpsheet 213 | Payments in kind – assets transferred |
| Helpsheet 252 | Capital allowances and balancing charges |

### For the *Self-employment* pages

| Helpsheet 204 | Limit on income tax reliefs |
|---|---|
| Helpsheet 220 | More than one business |
| Helpsheet 222 | How to calculate your taxable profits |
| Helpsheet 224 | Farmers and market gardeners |
| Helpsheet 227 | Losses |
| Helpsheet 229 | Information from your accounts |
| Helpsheet 232 | Farm and stock valuation |
| Helpsheet 234 | Averaging for creators of literary or artistic works |
| Helpsheet 236 | Qualifying care relief: foster carers, adult placement carers, kinship carers and staying put carers |
| Helpsheet 238 | Revenue recognition in service contracts – UITF 40 |
| Helpsheet 252 | Capital allowances and balancing charges |
| TH FS2 Self-Assessment | Using the three line account |

**For the *Lloyd's underwriters* pages**

| Helpsheet 240 | Lloyd's underwriters |
|---|---|

**For the *UK property* pages**

| Helpsheet 223 | Rent a Room for traders |
|---|---|
| Helpsheet 251 | Agricultural land |
| Helpsheet 252 | Capital allowances and balancing charges |
| Helpsheet 253 | Furnished Holiday Lettings |

**For the *Foreign* pages**

| Helpsheet 260 | Overlap |
|---|---|
| Helpsheet 261 | Foreign tax credit relief: capital gains |
| Helpsheet 262 | Income and benefits from transfers of assets abroad and income from non-resident trusts |
| Helpsheet 263 | Calculating foreign tax credit relief on income |
| Helpsheet 264 | Remittance basis |
| Helpsheet 321 | Gains on foreign life insurance policies |

**For the *Trusts etc.* pages**

| Helpsheet 270 | Trusts and settlements – income treated as the settlor's |
|---|---|

**For the *Capital gains summary* pages**

| Helpsheet 275 | Entrepreneurs' Relief |
|---|---|
| Helpsheet 276 | Incorporation Relief |
| Helpsheet 278 | Temporary non-residents and Capital Gains Tax |
| Helpsheet 281 | Husband and wife, civil partners, divorce, dissolution and separation |
| Helpsheet 282 | Death, personal representatives and legatees |
| Helpsheet 283 | Private Residence Relief |
| Helpsheet 284 | Shares and Capital Gains Tax |
| Helpsheet 285 | Share reorganisations, company takeovers and Capital Gains Tax |
| Helpsheet 286 | Negligible value claims and Income Tax losses on disposals of shares you have subscribed for in qualifying trading companies |
| Helpsheet 287 | Employee share and security schemes and Capital Gains Tax |

**For the *Residence, remittance basis etc.* pages**

 **Tax-planning dos**

- Buy your own home as soon as you can. Historically (i.e. over the long term), property has been a good investment. Any capital gain on your principal private residence will be tax free. However, by the same token, there are no tax allowances for any losses on sale.

- Make sure you have got good pension and life assurance cover and keep the situation constantly under review.

- Make use (if you can afford to) of the £3,000 tax-free annual capital transfer (i.e. give this sum away Inheritance-Tax-free each year) and if you did not use up last year's allowance, you can give away an additional £3,000.

- Always claim your personal and other tax allowances. This should normally be dealt with for you by HMRC, but you should keep the matter under annual review. For example, have you passed retirement age? This is relevant, because all sorts of considerations need to be taken into account, such as the fact that you will be receiving a state pension and you may continue working.

- Claim all business expenses you are entitled to against any business income – always keep a chit for petty cash expenses. If you don't, how will your accountant know you have incurred that particular expense?

- Pay your spouse properly for any work they do in your business. In the 2015/16 tax year, remember that they can earn £10,600 tax free, although payments over £8,060 will incur National Insurance Contributions.

- Consult with your stockbroker in order to make sure you take advantage of the annual £11,000 Capital Gains Tax exempt amount, i.e. if you can make a gain of this size, it will be tax free.

- Make a Will. You can create one inexpensively using Lawpack's *DIY Last Will & Testament Kit* or you can take legal advice.

- Think carefully about providing funds to pay any Inheritance Tax on death (term assurance isn't very expensive).

- Plan ahead and, wherever possible, let your accountant know in advance of your plans/wishes so that you can be advised on any tax implications.

- Divide your assets and income with your spouse or civil partner so that the best use is made of the independent taxation rules.

- Let an independent financial adviser give you the equivalent of a financial 'medical examination'.

- Ask your accountant to give a rough idea of your tax liability in January and July each year. Then divide the sum by 12 and start saving up for it by transferring the monthly figure to a deposit account. This way paying tax is much less painful.

- Transfer unused allowances between spouses/civil partners where circumstances permit.

## (101) Tax-planning don'ts

- Don't enter into tax-saving schemes, on the advice of either an accountant or anyone else, that run a long time. The law can change, your circumstances can change and either could make a nonsense of a long-term plan.

- Don't enter into highly complex or contrived tax-saving schemes without extremely careful thought and consideration. There is increasing public and political resistance to these schemes and they are the target of a lot of new and planned legislation. Participating in a scheme which fails could prove to be very expensive.

- Don't automatically trust trusts – refer to Lawpack's *Tax Answers at a Glance* book if you want more information on this matter. Be very careful about putting your money into trusts – don't set them up unless they will do exactly what you want. Trusts which are set up to protect assets from the ravages of tax can result not only in tax having to be paid, but also in assets having to be sold to pay the tax. The net result can be ghastly. Some trusts are very useful but tread very carefully – take professional advice.

- Don't give all your money away in order to save Inheritance Tax. If you do, what will you live on?

- Don't make your affairs too complicated. Keep your affairs simple and flexible so that you can (a) understand what is going on and (b) make any changes as and when you want.

- Don't try to cheat the taxman. Be honest in all your dealings. Keep proper records of all your transactions, especially cash receipts, and declare everything properly. If you don't, you will be found out.

## 2015/2016 Tax rates and allowances at a glance

### INCOME TAX

| BAND | FROM | TO | RATE |
|---|---|---|---|
| Starting Rate for Savings* | £0 | £5,000 | Nil |
| Basic Rate | £0 | £31,785 | 20% |
| Higher Rate | £31,786 | £150,000 | 40% |
| Additional Rate | £150,001 | | 45% |

*If your non-savings income is above this limit then the 0% starting rate will not apply.

In addition to the ordinary rate for dividends there is the 32.5% higher rate and 37.5% additional rate.

### CAPITAL GAINS TAX (for individuals)

| |
|---|
| First £11,100 exempt |
| 18% for standard rate payers, 28% for higher rate payers, (10% if Entrepreneurs' Relief applies) |

### CORPORATION TAX

| BAND | FROM | TO | RATE |
|---|---|---|---|
| Small Companies Rate | £1 | £300,000 | 20% |
| Marginal Relief | £300,001 | £1,500,000 | 20% |
| Main Rate | 1,500,001 | | 20% |

### INHERITANCE TAX (on death)

| BAND | FROM | TO | RATE |
|---|---|---|---|
| Nil Rate Band | £0 | £325,000 | 0% |
| Over Nil Rate Band | £325,001 | | 40% |

### PERSONAL ALLOWANCES

| | |
|---|---|
| Personal** | £10,600 |
| Personal (aged 65-74) | £10,600 |
| Personal (aged over 75) | £10,660 |
| Married Couples (aged over 75)*# | £8,355 |

All three higher age allowances are only available for incomes up to £27,00 for 2015/16

\* relief restricted to 10%

\# husband or wife must be born before 6 April 1935

\** The Personal Allowance reduces where income is above £100,000 - by £1 for every £2 of income over the £100,000 limit. This reduction applies irrespective of age.

### NATIONAL INSURANCE

| TYPE | EARNINGS PER WEEK | RATE |
|---|---|---|
| Class 1 (Employment) | *Employee (not contracted out)* | |
| | Up to £155 | Nil |
| | £155 to £815 | 12% |
| | Over £815 | 2% |
| | *Employer (not contracted out)* | |
| | Up to £156 | Nil |
| | Over £156 | 13.8% |

### NATIONAL INSURANCE (continued)

| TYPE | EARNINGS PER WEEK | RATE |
|---|---|---|
| Class 2 (Self-Employment) | (The old weekly stamp) | £2.80 |
| | No contributions due if profits below £5,965 | |
| Class 4 (Self-Employment) | 9% on profits between £8,060 and £42,385 | |
| | 2% on profits over £42,385 | |

### STATE PENSION

| | PER WEEK | PER YEAR |
|---|---|---|
| Single | £115.95 | £6,029.40 |
| Married | £185.45 | £9,643.40 |
| Age addition (over 80) | £0.25 | £13.00 |

### VAT

| | |
|---|---|
| Threshold with effect from 1 April | £82,000 |
| Rate | 20% |
| Annual accounting threshold | £1,350,000 |
| Cash accounting threshold | £1,350,000 |

### STAMP DUTY LAND TAX ON RESIDENTIAL PROPERTY

| From/to | 0 | £125,000 | Nil* |
|---|---|---|---|
| From/to | £125,001 | £250,000 | 2% |
| From/to | £250,001 | £925,000 | 5% |
| From/to | £925,001 | £1,500,000 | 10% |
| From | £1,500,001 | | 12% |
| Acquisition of residential property over £500,000 by 'non-natural persons' | | | 15% |

### TAXABLE CAR BENEFITS

| Car Benefit | The scale charge is based on CO$_2$ emissions. The annual charge ranges from 5% for eco-friendly cars to 35% for gas guzzlers. There is no adjustment for the age of car, nor for business mileage. Alternative rates apply to cars registered before 01.01.1998. Diesels attract a 3% surcharge, but not over 35%. Electric cars and vans have 0% benefit charge. |
|---|---|
| Fuel Benefit | As with Car Benefit, the taxable charge is based on CO$_2$ emissions. The charge is based on a sum of £22,100 for all cars, not on the price of the car. |
| Van Benefit | Any age of vehicle |
| | Van Scale Charge — £3,150 |
| | Fuel Scale Charge for Vans — £594 |

### CAR MILEAGE ALLOWANCE

All Engine Sizes

| | |
|---|---|
| Up to 10,000 miles pa | 45p |
| Over 10,000 miles pa | 25p |

## 2014/2015 Tax rates and allowances at a glance

### INCOME TAX

| BAND | FROM | TO | RATE |
|---|---|---|---|
| Starting Rate for Savings* | £0 | £2,880 | 10% |
| Basic Rate | £0 | £31,865 | 20% |
| Higher Rate | £31,866 | £150,000 | 40% |
| Additional Rate | £150,001 | | 50% |

*If your non-savings income is above this limit then the 10% starting rate will not apply.

In addition to the ordinary rate for dividends there is the 32.5% higher rate and 37.5% additional rate.

### CAPITAL GAINS TAX (for individuals)

| |
|---|
| First £11,000 exempt |
| 18% for standard rate payers, 28% for higher rate payers, (10% if Entrepreneurs' Relief applies) |

### CORPORATION TAX

| BAND | FROM | TO | RATE |
|---|---|---|---|
| Small Companies Rate | £1 | £300,000 | 20% |
| Marginal Relief | £300,001 | £1,500,000 | 21% |
| Main Rate | 1,500,001 | | 21% |

### INHERITANCE TAX (on death)

| BAND | FROM | TO | RATE |
|---|---|---|---|
| Nil Rate Band | £0 | £325,000 | 0% |
| Over Nil Rate Band | £325,001 | | 40% |

### PERSONAL ALLOWANCES

| | |
|---|---|
| Personal** | £10,000 |
| Personal (aged 65-74) | £10,500 |
| Personal (aged over 75) | £10,660 |
| Married Couples (aged over 75)*# | £8,165 |

All three higher age allowances are only available for incomes up to £27,000 for 2014/15

* relief restricted to 10%

# husband or wife must be born before 6 April 1935

** The Personal Allowance reduces where income is above £100,000 - by £1 for every £2 of income over the £100,000 limit. This reduction applies irrespective of age.

### NATIONAL INSURANCE

| TYPE | EARNINGS PER WEEK | RATE |
|---|---|---|
| Class 1 (Employment) | *Employee (not contracted out)* | |
| | Up to £153 | Nil |
| | £153 to £805 | 12% |
| | Over £805 | 2% |
| | *Employer (not contracted out)* | |
| | Up to £153 | Nil |
| | Over £153 | 13.8% |

### NATIONAL INSURANCE (continued)

| TYPE | EARNINGS PER WEEK | RATE |
|---|---|---|
| Class 2 (Self-Employment) | (The old weekly stamp) | £2.75 |
| | No contributions due if profits below £5,885 | |
| Class 4 (Self-Employment) | 9% on profits between £7,956 and £41,865 | |
| | 2% on profits over £41,865 | |

### STATE PENSION

| | PER WEEK | PER YEAR |
|---|---|---|
| Single | £113.10 | £5,881.20 |
| Married | £171.85 | £9,406.80 |
| Age addition (over 80) | £0.25 | £13.00 |

### VAT

| | |
|---|---|
| Threshold with effect from 1 April | £81,000 |
| Rate | 20% |
| Annual accounting threshold | £1,350,000 |
| Cash accounting threshold | £1,350,000 |

### STAMP DUTY LAND TAX ON RESIDENTIAL PROPERTY

| From/to | 0 | £125,000 | Nil* |
|---|---|---|---|
| From/to | £125,001 | £250,000 | 1% |
| From/to | £250,001 | £500,000 | 3% |
| From/to | £500,001 | £1,000,000 | 4% |
| From/to | £1,000,001 | £2,000,000 | 5% |
| From | £2,000,001 | | 7% |

| | |
|---|---|
| Acquisition of residential property over £500,000 by 'non-natural persons' | 15% |

### TAXABLE CAR BENEFITS

| Car Benefit | The scale charge is based on $CO_2$ emissions. The annual charge ranges from 5% for eco-friendly cars to 35% for gas guzzlers. There is no adjustment for the age of car, nor for business mileage. Alternative rates apply to cars registered before 01.01.1998. Diesels attract a 3% surcharge, but not over 35%. Electric cars and vans have 0% benefit charge. |
|---|---|
| Fuel Benefit | As with Car Benefit, the taxable charge is based on $CO_2$ emissions. The charge is based on a sum of £21,700 for all cars, not on the price of the car. |

| Van Benefit | Any age of vehicle | |
|---|---|---|
| | Van Scale Charge | £3,090 |
| | Fuel Scale Charge for Vans | £581 |

### CAR MILEAGE ALLOWANCE

All Engine Sizes

| | |
|---|---|
| Up to 10,000 miles pa | 45p |
| Over 10,000 miles pa | 25p |

## VAT fuel scale charges for three-month periods

| CO$_2$ band | VAT Fuel Scale Charge, 3-month period £ | VAT on 3-month charge £ | VAT exclusive 3-month charge £ |
|---|---|---|---|
| 120 or less | 156.00 | 26.00 | 130.00 |
| 125 | 234.00 | 39.00 | 195.00 |
| 130 | 251.00 | 41.83 | 209.17 |
| 135 | 266.00 | 44.33 | 221.67 |
| 140 | 282.00 | 47.00 | 235.00 |
| 145 | 297.00 | 49.50 | 247.50 |
| 150 | 313.00 | 52.17 | 260.83 |
| 155 | 328.00 | 54.67 | 273.33 |
| 160 | 345.00 | 57.50 | 287.50 |
| 165 | 360.00 | 60.00 | 300.00 |
| 170 | 376.00 | 62.67 | 313.33 |
| 175 | 391.00 | 65.17 | 325.83 |
| 180 | 408.00 | 68.00 | 340.00 |
| 185 | 423.00 | 70.50 | 352.50 |
| 190 | 439.00 | 73.17 | 365.83 |
| 195 | 454.00 | 75.67 | 378.33 |
| 200 | 470.00 | 78.33 | 391.67 |
| 205 | 485.00 | 80.83 | 404.17 |
| 210 | 502.00 | 83.67 | 418.33 |
| 215 | 517.00 | 86.17 | 430.83 |
| 220 | 533.00 | 88.83 | 444.17 |
| 225 or more | 548.00 | 91.33 | 456.67 |

Where the CO$_2$ emission figure is not a multiple of 5, the figure is rounded down to the next multiple of 5 to determine the level of the charge. For a bi-fuel vehicle which has two CO$_2$ emissions figures, the lower of the two figures should be used. For cars which are too old to have a CO$_2$ emissions figure, you should identify the CO$_2$ band based on engine size, as follows:

If its cylinder capacity is 1,400cc or less, use CO$_2$ band 140.

If its cylinder capacity exceeds 1,400cc but does not exceed 2,000cc, use CO$_2$ band 175.

If its cylinder capacity exceeds 2,000cc, use CO$_2$ band 225 or above.

**Template form proving that your spouse/civil partner genuinely works in your business**

**Agreement between:**

_____

**and**

_____

We, the undersigned, agree that my wife/husband/civil partner undertakes responsibility for the following activities in my business:

_____

_____

_____

_____

_____

_____

_____

It is agreed that for these services my wife/husband/civil partner will receive the sum of £_____ per year to be paid monthly.

This arrangement is effective from _____

_____

Signed: _____Proprietor

Signed: _____Wife/Husband/Civil partner

Dated: _____

# Index

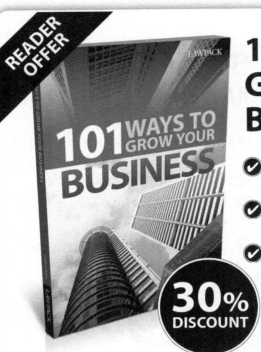